daughter

**A GIRL-TO-GIRL CONVERSATION
ABOUT WHAT IT MEANS TO BE ONE**

DEBORAH ISABEL MILLER

Editor: Janessa Miller

Photos: Val Stoltzfus

Models: Dave Miller and his daughter Deborah
Ben Yoder and his daughters Zoe and Olivia

Photo location: Old House Love Company

Designed and printed by:

SCHLABACH PRINTERS
Sugarcreek, OH
schlabachprinters.com

To Mom and Dad,

Thank you for exemplifying the way of honor

and making God's love so believable.

CONTENTS

foreword

BY DAVE MILLER

*And he will turn the hearts of fathers to their children
and the hearts of children to their fathers.*
Malachi 4:6

I have been moved to tears as I paged from chapter to chapter of this book. My daughter Deborah's illustrations and stories of our relationship brought back many memories, some of which I had forgotten. There were many good memories as I realized how those early years of our relationship had formed her life and how much she wanted to be like her daddy.

But I was also taken back to moments of hard conversations as I learned the Malachi 4:6 principle of winning my daughter's heart. There was a point when I felt like her peers had more influence in her life than I did. I began to pray and ask God for wisdom about how to walk through this. It became clear that she felt a critical spirit from me. In contrast, when Deborah went to her peers, they affirmed her. Guess who had the greater influence?

After discovering this critical spirit in my life, I repented. I began to be intentional about speaking words of blessing and life to my daughter instead of criticism. I quickly learned that this was a much more effective way to parent than focusing on the negative.

James 3:10 says, "Out of the same mouth proceedeth blessing and cursing. My brethren, these things ought not so to be" (KJV).

Proverbs 18:21 says, "Death and life are in the power of the tongue: and they that love it shall eat the fruit thereof" (KJV).

While I was learning these principles, God was working on my daughter's heart as well, teaching her how to relate to me. Together we continued seeking the Lord about how to best nurture our relationship. You will learn that neither of us was perfect, nor did we always respond correctly. However, years later, our relationship is beyond what we could have imagined.

The original vision for this book was birthed from young ladies approaching my daughter about their own relationships with their dads. I believe many young ladies will benefit from the practical advice Deborah gives. And if a dad picks it up to check it out, I believe he will also be encouraged and challenged.

Writing this book was not an easy process and much of it was done in between ministry tours. I remember one tearful call from Deborah when she was spending a week with her editor. She wondered whether it was worth finishing the book. After hearing her out, I assured her that what God had placed in her heart was worth completing, and her mom and I would stand with her through it.

She would often ask me how she should prioritize her time. Should she go out with a friend or stay back and work on the book? Then there were precious moments of holding her in my arms. Late night talks when she wasn't sure if she had what it took or if this book would even be worth reading. She would cry on my shoulder, asking for wisdom. These are moments I will forever cherish.

What you read in these pages is real life. We have nothing to hide. I have been very blessed and challenged in watching my daughter process life through the words of this book, and I endorse the entirety of its content. I trust it will be used as a tool to restore and deepen relationships.

Deborah, I am so proud of you for putting yourself out there, for all the hours of hard work, and for your faithfulness to Jesus. I love you, sweet girl.

Dave Miller
Executive Director, Gospel Express Ministries
Deborah's Dad

champion

A NOTE TO THE DAUGHTERS WHO HAVE
BEEN ABUSED, MISUSED, OR MANIPULATED

Mom pulled out the language book and handed it to my little sister as we were traveling in our bus-and-trailer entourage, headed who knows where. My sister groaned and begged to please skip language class today. Just today.

I sympathized with her pleas for mercy. Trying to get schoolwork done while traveling was such a chore for me when I was her age. She continued to make touching appeals to my mom's soft spots, but Mom knew this wasn't the first day they had skipped, so she stuck to her plan. Language class started, but my sister found many convenient distractions to avoid the pain at hand.

My mom exuberantly read the lesson to my sister, trying to keep her focused and excited. She said brightly, "Did you catch that? They're giving you a secret for life!"

My sister replied, "The secret to life? You're telling me that this will help me for all the situations I'll face in life? What if I get kidnapped? How will I know how to escape? How will this help me then?"

Mom saw her game and kindly tried to refocus her, but my sister wouldn't give up the convenient distraction. She said, and I quote, "What if they take me and tell me they're going to kill me?"

Mom laid down her teacher's guide and with both charm and warning replied, "Then you would know that the verb is *kill*."

However off subject my sister was, she had this right: lessons on verbs don't always translate well to traumatic kidnappings. And lessons in relationships don't always translate well to traumatic stories. This book was written mainly for girls who have good-hearted dads, even if their dads aren't perfect. So if you filter the content through the lens of an absent, neglectful, manipulative, or in any way abusive dad, it may be taken wrongly.

If that is your story, I just want to take a minute to talk about the vital place you have in this conversation.

Dads sometimes make horrible choices that devastate or damage the lives of their daughters. I can think of few things more unjust than innocent girls who are left alone, taken advantage of, or manipulated. It is especially heinous when done in the name of religion. Beth Moore said about her own life, "In my most fundamental years, the person I needed to trust the most was the person I could trust the least. When protectors turn to perpetrators, nothing comes harder for us."[1]

Nothing comes harder. When our safe places become unsafe, it seems like nothing in the world can be trusted. Some of the stories girls have told me about themselves and their dads clearly show that there is something wrong with this world.

I remember leaning in close to hear a girl talk about the anger and control directed toward her under the banner of obeying God. Her father's behavior was wrong on more levels than I can begin to express. When I listened to my friend talk about how abuse felt normal, because she knew nothing else, I felt a kind of numb question: *How can this be?* There are some things I can't make sense of. We know this is not how things were meant to be, but because of sin, this is exactly how they are.

Our sin-cursed world sets us up for a lot of disappointment, pain, and injustice. Inside we know, something is wrong. We weren't meant to live like this. We weren't meant to treat each other like this.

We are beings created for Eden. A place where fellowship with God, and each other, is pure, peaceful, and pleasurable. Where the food we eat doesn't rot, carry diseases, or have to be approved by the FDA. A place where there is no pollution, in the air or our minds, and where motives are as good as our grandmas' recipes. A place where people are fully alive and stay alive. Where our feelings are freely and naturally harmonizing with the truth.

But we aren't in Eden anymore, are we?

God created us for Eden. He never wanted us to be hurt. He wants us to be whole and alive. But we know how the story of Eden ends: fruit, snake, woman, man, lies, and a choice—to believe those lies and act on them.[2] Humankind was beautifully created in God's image, which means we were given the freedom of choice, just as He has free choice. Adam and Eve made a devastating choice with this freedom.

Then there was a different garden, the same snake, and more lies.[3] But this time, Jesus was there. And He made a choice to believe what His Father said was true. A choice to take the consequences of *our* bad choices on His innocent self. All this madness was placed onto the only one who had nothing to do with the mess: God.

The Cross gave each of us an invitation back to full restoration, freedom, peace, and connection with God. A connection so close that He adopts us into His own household. Daughter status.

THE IN-BETWEEN

This is the truth, but we aren't in heaven, where this truth can be seen with our eyes. We are in the awkward in-between. Something of an adolescent, gap-year, light-jacket, transition season between the Cross and heaven. All we see with our physical eyes is our fallen world, where people have hurt us and lies are even more numerous than our personal selfie collections. In this in-between world, it's what we do with the Cross that will determine how we live our lives and spend eternity.

Believing God invites the reality and redemption of the Cross into our everyday lives. The only power Satan has over our souls comes when we agree with one of his lies. In heaven, we will clearly know truth. But while we await the return of Christ, every single person must wrestle between the lies and pain of this fallen world and the truth of what God has already done. We live in a time where the finished work of the Cross is not yet seen with our physical eyes. It must be believed, in faith, with our spiritual eyes. But one day our faith will become sight. Our suffering will become gold. Our crosses will become crowns.

Sometimes daughters can't do anything about their dad's choices. They can't rewrite the story. They can't know if their dad will ever change or become safe in the future. The free-will choice of human-kind, and the decay of death in our world, will sometimes leave us in situations where it seems like we can't do anything.

We cannot change what happened to us or the choices of other people. But because of the Cross, we can receive God's freeing, finished redemption for our situation. We can hope, knowing He will one day make all things new (Revelation 21:5).

Before that day comes, here are some ways you can reach toward the personal healing and redemption God offers, even if you can't change anything about your relationship with your dad.

WHAT YOU CAN DO WHEN IT SEEMS LIKE THERE'S NOTHING YOU CAN DO.

1. Tell Someone the Truth

Talking about abuse and misuse is hard. It can involve legalities, rejection, and facing shame that would feel easier to hide away.

Recently, I sat in a coffee shop with a group of ladies, listening as my friend shared about her own story of abuse. She had sworn to never tell. But one day she did. She had no idea that the person she confided in was legally obligated to act on the information. As the facts became known, my friend had to face hard circumstances.

But she said the relief she felt was unbelievable. All her life, this secret had made her wonder if anyone would ever love her if they knew. And now, everyone knew. And not all, but most people, loved and understood her more than they had before. She finally knew that she didn't have to hide pieces of her story in order to be loved. Yes, there was pain involved. But this girl is a different woman now, no longer defined by her dad's choices. No longer needing to hide. She would not be where she is today if she had kept this all a secret.

Another reason girls may not speak about abuse, manipulation, or control is because it's their normal. Often people are first mistreated when they are too young to know how to make it stop. All of us have places and relationships that make up our definition of "normal." When our normal feels shameful, we can be blinded to the truth that our homes and relationships were meant to feel healthy and safe. It is not everyone's normal to be violated, shut down, or taken advantage of behind closed doors.

If any kind of abuse has become your normal, it shouldn't be. No matter your situation, seek someone to talk to about what's going on at home. If you aren't sure if your situation is actually *that bad,* but something in you feels scared by this request, please talk. Even if it feels like it could ruin everything, you will never be fully free until what's hidden becomes known.

Another reason some girls keep their mouths shut is because they think it's their fault. Whatever sin their dad has done, somehow the enemy has twisted the situation into shameful lies about the girl. There is no room for abuse, neglect, or manipulation on an authority's part, no matter what you did or didn't do. There are absolutely no excuses. You don't have to justify your dad's actions. You don't have to try to fix it or believe you could have done something better. Your dad's sin is not your fault.

You do not have to shoulder the weight of your dad's sin alone or try to protect your family by keeping things quiet. This is not your job. Allow yourself to be honest with someone who can help you navigate this situation you were not meant to carry. Even if it gets messy in the process, keeping things hidden has never brought anyone real freedom, you and your dad included. You are free to be honest.

2. Get Whatever Help You Need

Words like "counseling" or "mentors" can sound a little scary, depending on how you've seen them play out around you. But you truly don't have to go on living with the effects of wrongs others have done to you. There are people who can help you. They cannot set you free themselves, but they can lead you to Jesus when you can't make heads or tails of confusing emotions or memories on your own. They can ask you wise questions, unpacking the lies that keep you locked into past circumstances. They can help you set up boundaries to stop abuse or manipulation.

I myself have benefited so much from counseling. Partly because the people I've received counseling from are biblically-grounded and Spirit-led. They allow themselves to be used to get me past myself and into the presence of Jesus. Not all counseling is like this. Not all mentors or accountability partners will be equipped to help you. But there are those who can. If you find yourself stuck, allow yourself to be carried to Christ by the godly help of others.

People won't be your healers, but God made us with a built-in need for community. You don't need to try to navigate your situation alone. But, ultimately, it is the gospel that will bring your freedom. Cling to Christ. Read His Word like it's your lifeline. Get in His presence. Do whatever it takes to touch the hem of His garment and come to full healing. He has done all the work for you to be completely whole. It's up to you to choose to come into agreement with this truth, doing what it takes to get there.

3. Look for Good Authorities

If you have a bad taste in your mouth from your dad's leadership or lack thereof, it may be instinctive to avoid leadership and authorities in general, to try to spare yourself from repeated pain. But greater healing may come to your heart if you intentionally seek to place yourself under healthy, godly authorities.

So how does this look? First, ask yourself if you have a tendency to despise authority instead of welcoming it. You may already have loving authority figures available around you. Are you subconsciously rejecting them because of past hurts?

Second, understand that you are pursuing a heart condition more than a dad replacement. Ask God to nurture within you the heart of a daughter who knows the warmth, safety, and courage of submission to authority.

Then look for opportunities to connect with healthy authorities. Plug into a church, ministry, or place of business where you can practice honor for authority. Where you can learn what it's like for someone to look out for you, give you counsel, and teach you to honor their ideas, when they may not jive with your own. God wants you to know the stability of submission to authorities and father figures in your life. He wants to be a Father to you, even if you can't be close to your own.

YOUR PLACE IN THIS CONVERSATION

Since this book is written primarily to girls with good-hearted dads, if your story sounds more like a traumatic kidnapping than a midday language class, it may feel hard to know where your spot is in this conversation. In my mind, your place is in the center of the podium, holding the bouquet as a gold medal is strung around your neck.

When I see you believing in the power of the Cross to redeem how others' bad choices have affected your life, I start getting ready for the awards ceremony. When I see God making you whole, restoring what was taken from you, and putting that sparkle back in your eyes, I feel like I'm Gilbert Blythe in that *Anne of Green Gables* scene where he claps like a madman and jumps to his feet after her recitation of "The Highwayman."[4] Heaven only knows the rewards you will receive when you arrive there.

I know that our just God knows the injustices done to you. He sees every tearful, gritty, broken moment, and He will create gold out of every part of the story you hand to Him. You may stand on that podium with sweat and dirt and deep heaves of relief, like champion athletes do, but you will stand having run your race with endurance. Without a doubt, I will be in your corner, ecstatic with clapping and cheers, as I watch God string the gold medal over your neck. You are the real champion in this conversation.

BEFORE YOU READ THIS BOOK

I have a few things I'd like to share, from one girl to another. I'll start by saying, it's pretty scary for me to publish this book. It feels risky to put my words and stories in the hands of others. I know I may be wrong. I know I won't say things perfectly. I know I'm fairly young to have written a book, which means my writing skill set and life experience have much room for growth. I am still forming my fundamental values, life goals, theology, and learning a ton about relationships. So sharing from where I'm at now is a vulnerable act of faith. My dad and I are still learning many of the concepts talked about in these chapters. My greatest fear is that someone would take content from this book and require an ideal, a standard, or an expectation of themselves that God and His Word does not require of them.

So please don't read this book as the gospel. Read it as a testimony from an imperfect girl, talking about how the gospel impacts our lives, stories, and relationships.

I am finding that, in the end, it is the gospel that keeps my relationships the healthiest. Not personality tests and podcasts. Not conferences and Bible schools. Not relationship books like this one. All these things have their place. But the most lasting, powerful thing that will keep us walking like Jesus is the gospel that moves us into a new way of living and relating.

A book written by an imperfect girl is only a reminder that the gospel is continually working to change our lives and relationships.

OUR DAD'S ROLE

In this book, we will talk about what it means to be a daughter to God and to our dads. We'll discuss how our dads affect our lives and our view of God, and how we affect theirs. We'll open conversations about good communication and connection. We'll talk about the power of honor and healthy processing. Mainly, we will talk about how we can be faithful in our role as daughters. Faithful being the key word here, because it's what Jesus seems to be on the lookout for, saying, "Well done, good and faithful servant" (Matthew 25:23).

We'll talk about how we can be faithful with our role, but, before we do, I want to acknowledge that there may be some reading this who have not experienced good dads.

If your story with your dad has been difficult, I want to take a moment to say, I'm sorry.

Some of you may have lost your father—so even if he was a great dad, you no longer have the warmth of his presence in your life. If you've lost your dad, I grieve with you.

For those of you with unsaved fathers, I want to applaud the courage it takes to stand for Christ when someone in your own household may not be standing with you. Jesus said this will happen: "For I have come to set a man against his father, and a daughter against her mother. . . . And a person's enemies will be those of his own household. Whoever loves father or mother more than me is not worthy of me" (Matthew 10:35–37).

If your dad has not stood for Christ with you or represented Christ to you, Jesus sees and applauds you for choosing Him above all else.

If you have put effort into honoring your dad, but he hasn't put effort into loving you, I know this matters to God.

If your dad has valued you for what you do more than who you are, I'm sorry.

If your father has been absent or left your family, I can only imagine how hard this must be.

If your relationship with your dad hasn't been a safe place, I'm sure this loss isn't easy to live with.

If your dad has spent far more time correcting and corralling your dreams and gifts than affirming and valuing them, I believe the heart of God is grieved.

Because of the position of leadership God has given our dads, He holds them to a high accountability in their role. He wants them to be the ones loving us before we learn to love them back. He wants them to be the ones calling us to life before we know how to return the favor. In a fallen world, it won't always be this way, and I want to give you permission to grieve and acknowledge your dad's choices for what they are.

Our own faithfulness as daughters does not diminish anything about our dad's role and what God requires of him. But faithfulness may remind us not to use our dad's choices as excuses for sin or wrong attitudes in our own lives.

BEING FAITHFUL WITH OUR ROLE

Being faithful does not mean taking control of the relationships around us until we have forced them to fit our ideals. Faithfulness is tending to what we've been given. This means one person's relationship with her dad may look vastly different than the next, because they've been given a different set of personalities, circumstances, losses, and blessings. Sometimes the most faithful step to take is withholding words. Other times it's communicating. Sometimes the faithful step is giving space in the relationship. Other times it means moving in closer. I don't believe God asks us to follow a formula in our relationships, but I do believe He asks for intentionality.

As you read this book, frame it with this simple question: "God, how can I be faithful with my story?" This book is written mainly to girls with good-hearted dads, which means some content won't apply to all situations. You don't need to practice or agree with all the concepts discussed in this book, you simply need to tend the relationship God gave you. Ask Him what it looks like to be faithful. In this faithfulness, be at rest.

A friend of mine who lost her dad when she was young told me, "I didn't know how to have a dad. I didn't know how to be at rest. But then I realized I don't have to try to be a daughter. I *am* a daughter."

If you know the cross-crucified Jesus, then you already are a daughter. You already have the full-blown benefits, confidence, provision, and love of a good Father whose name is God. He will give you what you need to be faithful with your story and your dad.

NOTHING COMPARES TO BEING

TRULY, EXUBERANTLY

wanted

BY YOUR CHILDREN.

FRANCIS CHAN[1]

CHAPTER 1

father

A GOD WHO NAMED HIMSELF THAT

Dad called me his bright-eyed, dreamy, twirly "little Betsy." In those simple childhood days, the two of us thrived on "welcome home" hugs, bedtime tickles, runs across the yard yelling "catch me," and that flight to the sky as he'd toss me into the air. But as I grew older, those simple days began to morph into more complicated ones. I didn't even notice what was happening until, one night, I was forced to recognize the change.

On that night, I was attending a women's event. We were all gathered in a gym, decorated to try and make up for the fluorescent lights and basketball hoops overhead. I scanned the room with my young eyes. There was the solemn-faced lady with the kinky hair pulled into a neat bun. There was the pastor's wife and a group of teenagers in pretty dresses. Then there was me, sitting among them in an outfit my mom had picked out, which I wasn't a big fan of. I felt small as I watched the faces of all the adult women around me.

My mom was the speaker for this event, which is why I found myself among these women in the first place. At the end of her session, she gave the ladies a pamphlet to take home to their husbands. It contained questions and spaces for feedback to help them open up some needed conversations. The questions were worded in a way that could be used for multiple types of relationships, and since there were a few unmarried women in the room, she suggested trying out this pamphlet with our dads.

Once my mom and I got back out to the motorhome we were traveling in at the time, I handed my dad the pamphlet and asked him to fill it out. He gladly did. There were spaces for positive feedback and questions that helped him express his love in words. Then, at the bottom of the pamphlet, there was a space for some honest feedback about things that negatively affected our relationship.

The warm lights in the motorhome were being turned off and my siblings were crawling into their bunks when my dad handed the pamphlet back to me. I stood by the end of the tiny kitchen counter to read it, catching the light from the mounted lamp at the edge of the cabinets.

My heart sank when I reached the bottom of the pamphlet. After the cue statement, "I am hurt when you . . ." Dad had written, "Roll your eyes in response to me, have resentment in your voice when you talk to me, give me disapproving looks . . ."

A sadness came over me as I read these words. I had never stopped to consider that I could affect my dad negatively. I had never asked myself why subtle tension was developing between us, why my heart was sometimes closed to him, or why I reacted to him in resentment.

I felt confused. Could I do anything about this? We had a nice enough relationship, but I suddenly wished we could have more connection. My dad's words implied that he wished for it too.

But what were we supposed to do? In that stage of life, my dad didn't know how to win back the girl whose heart was closing off to his. I, in turn, hardly knew why my heart was closed off or what I could do about it. In that moment, I vowed to be a better daughter, but I didn't really know how.

It was in that same preteen stage when a young woman gave me a thoughtful offer. I remember watching her make her way toward me after a Sunday service. She was tall and pretty and somewhere in that awesome age between sixteen and eighteen.

Do you remember how girls that age seemed when you were a

preteen? They were my dreams embodied. And when they took notice of me, complimented me, or gave me even as much as a smile, I was sure my hope of becoming like them was that much closer. This girl walked straight up to me in the clustered crowd, placed a gentle hand on my shoulder, and began a kind conversation.

She told me that she understood what it was like to have questions about relationships with people in our own household. She sympathized that there were many reasons why it's tough to be a girl in this stage of life. She offered me her presence. "If you ever need someone to talk to about this girl stuff, give me a call!"

I had never been given an offer like this. And you know what I did with it? Nothing.

When she left me after that conversation, I wondered what I would even talk to her about. I was young enough that I hadn't thought much about life or how it was affecting me. I was just living it. Yet I was also starting to have some questions about who I was, facing some fears about love and acceptance, and feeling some new emotions in my relationship with my dad. Attempting to communicate any of this felt harder than letting it all sit inside me.

I regret not taking her up on her offer. I needed a girl like this even more than I needed Proactiv° acne solution. As I was emerging from the life of a carefree girl, it would have been so helpful to have someone guide me through the complexities of relationship struggles and desires I hadn't faced before. But, at the time, I didn't have words for a conversation like that. And I didn't consider the blessing of having someone help me find them.

More than a decade later, I'm grateful to say I have met many beautiful women who have helped me find words in the different stages of life I've faced. These different stages have held questions about God, boys, siblings, friendships, decisions, values, and, as we'll talk about in the remainder of this book, my relationship with my dad.

These women have taught me that offering an honest story and starting a conversation has the power to open someone's heart. As they have offered their presence in my life, I've been surprised by the one thing they don't do: they don't give me answers. They don't tell me what to do. Instead, they ask me questions, tell me about their own stories, and speak truth. Then they let me sit in my questions and make my own choices. They point me to Christ and assume finding Him will direct my steps, choices, and healing.

This almost makes me mad sometimes. I want hard facts and solid answers. *Please, just tell me what to do and how to do it.* But I wouldn't have it any other way. They know each story is different, each personality has its own vices, and each girl has her own choices. So they steer clear of a formula and offer me the transforming power of truth through the person of Jesus Christ and the warmth of their presence.

A lot has changed since those confusing preteen days. If my dad and I filled out these kinds of pamphlets today, we would still have plenty to say in that bottom section. But we now have a sense of safety, connection, and love that helps us work through any confusion or unresolved conflict. This is not because I figured out how to be a better daughter. It's because God has begun to teach me what it *means* to be a daughter.

My dad has also learned more about what it means to be a father. When my dad talks to men, he calls them to display a clear vision of what God means when He calls Himself our Father. Because my dad is a father, he calls fathers to do their job. And because I am a daughter, I will call us together to be faithful with our job as daughters. Even when our fathers haven't given us a clear vision of God as Father, we still have the opportunity to be faithful with the stories we have and experience what God says about Himself as a Father.

In this book, I have endeavored to study the subject of a dad and his girl in ways that will unpack the nature of God and what He has to say about us and our dads. But, beyond that, I hope to be a presence in your process. I hope to do this by offering a conversation about my own process and the process of other girls I've met. The kinds of conversations that my friends and mentors have with me.

Not to-dos or how-tos, but stories from lessons learned the hard way. Questions that were once voiceless, now understood. Fears that were stuffed down, then transformed. Lies that were controlling underneath layers of learned performance, now exposed. Embarrassing attempts at connection that flopped, then got touched by redemption. I hope to give you the permission to have your own questions, overcome your own fears, know God as Father, and embrace your own story of you and your dad.

WHO IS GOD?

Each of us has a story about us and our dads. With each story, there are most likely personalized questions about how to build a strong relationship. Some relationships come more naturally than others, but even in good situations, we sometimes run into unknowns that leave us without clear answers. We wonder what or who is wrong and how we can do anything about it.

Recently, a friend of mine voiced a good question about her own relationship with her dad. She was the pastor's daughter at a church our family was visiting. Pulling up a chair beside me over Sunday lunch, she started the conversation with, "So, I hear you're writing a book about father-daughter relationships!"

I cringed a little. I often wonder how many people would read a book about this. Surely, it's not actually that big of a deal? But just as I was in the middle of downplaying the book and saying that she's probably one of those girls who has a great relationship with her dad, she stopped me and said, "No, that's what I wanted to talk to you about. I do have a great dad. But I still struggle with our relationship sometimes. I know he's a way better dad than most of my friends have, and that's why I feel so bad. Am I just being ungrateful or discontent?"

Our conversation was interrupted before we could talk further. But I pondered her words. Are girls with good dads being discontent when they struggle to connect or relate with their dads?

Another friend of mine asked me, "How do I know when I'm honoring my father? I really want to honor him, but he never gives me feedback unless it's negative. It feels like I'll never be able to know when I'm honoring my dad."

These are good, valid questions. Questions we will discuss in the chapters ahead. But before we try to answer these questions, I think we need to ask even better ones. Questions like, "Who is God?" and "What would my life and relationships look like if I believed the answer to that question?"

A. W. Tozer said, "The most important thing about you is what you think about God."[2] All throughout the Bible, we see God answering people's questions by telling them about Himself. Because no matter how good or bad our dads are, no matter what our stories are like, our questions and cravings won't quit until we understand who He is and how that defines who we are.

MAKING SENSE OF OUR CRAVINGS FOR A DAD

Tossing her blonde curls, my little cousin called me, the babysitter, into her pink room and explained in her singsong voice, "Daddy says I'm the most beautiful dancer in the world. Watch!"

I leaned against the door to watch the performance. She hopped around in less-than-fluid motions, barely dodging the play kitchen and table that gave structure to her imaginary world. There was no rhyme or rhythm to go with her routine, but she oozed with the confidence of a master in her art. I quickly saw her dad's perspective was biased. But she really believed him, because she deemed him the most credible voice in her life.

When I was my little cousin's age, I had my own pretend kitchen and a purple bedroom, lovingly sponge-painted by my dad. Some of my favorite childhood memories were in that old home in the foothills of North Carolina's Blue Ridges. I remember one muggy Sunday evening, the boys were playing baseball in the yard, while sets of parents filled the dining room with stories and laughter. And my friends and I, the little girls, climbed the magnolia tree in our front lawn.

Perched on branches, one friend and I tried to one-up each other with a classic argument of "my dad is stronger than your dad." Clearly, I'd have the upper hand in our friendship if my dad could beat up her dad (as though our coffee-sipping, joke-telling fathers would put up fists).

"Which dad is older?" we asked, because in that stage of life, age equaled power. Then we compared and exaggerated scenarios about their work, how fast they could run, and how quickly they could cut down a tree or throw a ball.

My friend was a cool kid from out of town, while this home, friend group, and mature magnolia were my turf. Neither of us knew how to feel about the other, so this conversation was helping us lay down the lines of value and power. It came down to this: if my protector is stronger than your protector, then I am the better woman.

My cousin and I made it obvious: it's natural for little girls to want to be protected, valued, and enjoyed by a good dad. Bob Carlisle unwraps this natural craving in his song "Butterfly Kisses," which he wrote for his daughter's sixteenth birthday. The song tells the story of a dad watching his girl become a woman and their relationship in each stage of that process. I can hardly listen to it without tearing up. It communicates the kind of connection that, if missing, would make this song hard to hear.

Bob Carlisle once said, "I get a lot of mail from young girls who try to get me to marry their moms. That used to be a real chuckle because it's so cute, but then I realized: they don't want a romance for Mom. They want the father that's in that song. And that just kills me."[3]

Bob found some beautiful words for the connection between a father and his daughter, and it clicked for these little girls immediately. They knew it was missing.

When we're missing something, often all we feel is a void, a need, or a craving, but we don't know why it's there. If we seek to have these healthy cravings met in unhealthy ways, they will begin to drive and motivate our lives unknowingly. We all want to know if we're worth protecting and fighting for. We long to be understood and accepted, even with all our faults and weaknesses. We all desire to have someone call out our signature value. We want to know if we are in some way thrilling or lovable.

My cousin naturally assumed that her dad was the best person to show her that she was delightful. My out-of-state competition and I didn't need psychology classes to tell us our longing for value could be met by being fought for and protected. We both knew well enough on our own. And those little girls who wrote letters to Bob Carlisle didn't need to be told that the dad in that song was what they were craving. They reached for it as easily as we reach for a piece of candy, even if we've never tasted it before.

Have you ever wondered why we have this craving? I have wondered this as I've watched fully grown, capable women weep when they let themselves notice the fatherly love they never had. I remember sitting with one woman, crying soft tears as she pondered a painful incident she'd just had with her dad. After some time, she looked up at me and said softly, "I guess no matter how old you get, a girl still wants her dad's approval."

I had no idea what to say to her sweet, honest words. *Why would God put us in such a vulnerable position,* I wondered. *Why did He create us to long for a fatherly love so strongly?*

We could ask the same questions about moms and our need for nurture. About romance and our craving for it. About siblings and our longing for connection. About church and friends and our desire for community. Why would God make us with so much risk to be hurt by any of these relationships?

I don't presume to speak on behalf of God, but I do believe that there is a much bigger point to all this. Our cravings for relationship show us the character of our relational God.

A RELATIONAL GOD

God uses many things to describe Himself throughout the Bible. He uses words like lion, lamb, mother, brother, shepherd, counselor, governor, king, servant, friend, and groom. He does this to draw a picture of who He is, to help us understand His character and ways.

Everything God created here on earth somehow reflects a part of who He is, making Him believable. He artfully gave us pictures of Himself through the beauty

> WHEN WE ENGAGE IN ANY TYPE OF RELATIONSHIP, WE ARE EITHER POINTING TOWARD OR AWAY FROM A PART OF WHO GOD IS.

of the earth, the wonder of the galaxies, and the mystery of relationships. When we engage in any type of relationship, we are either pointing toward or away from a part of who God is.

And one thing God names Himself, over and over, is "Father."

A girl and her dad point to a relationship full of reverence, stability, affection, delight, obedience, laughter, and unconditional love. God meant this relationship to make that kind of connection believable when people encounter Him. As Lisa Chan said, "Our lives should make it believable that there is a God."[4]

The way my dad smiles at me with obvious thrill gives me a picture of what it's like to look into the face of God. The way he teases and enjoys me makes the affection of God understandable. When my dad compliments, affirms, blesses, and simply loves being around me, it helps me understand God in a way that seems too good to be true. I am twenty-five years old, and my dad still invites me onto his lap, holding me as I face the realities of a hard, broken world. He makes the "God of all comfort"[5] so believable.

The love, tickles, fun, hugs, praise, affection, counsel, and correction of my dad have brought me to a simple conclusion: if I can experience this here in a fallen world, then heaven must have an even better version.

But it took me a while to reach this conclusion, because I spent years letting these gifts keep me from truly knowing God in the same ways. I could hardly believe a holy God would love me like my dad did, because a holy God could see my flaws in a way my dad couldn't.

On the flip side, there were also some hard aspects of my relationship with my dad that skewed how I viewed God. I allowed my own perceptions and hurts to blind me from what I truly believed about God and how I related to Him.

God's original intent for relationships was perfectly good, life-giving, and beautiful. He never intended for us to be left bleeding or lacking in our relationships. Because sin entered the story, we now have imperfect relationships. The good news is: He restored the broken connection in our relationship with Him through the Cross. He did what it took to give us access to Himself as Father and to be satisfied instead of starving in our relationships.

Because we are still in this fallen world and mid-sanctification, no father will give us a picture-perfect vision of our relational God.

The saddest thing we could do with this reality is allow our earthly experience to keep us from knowing the Fatherly character of God personally. And there is another reality: our fathers don't usually get it all wrong either. I hope we can learn to live more gratefully for those places they showed us something remarkable about our God, because relationship with Him is ultimately what we crave.

THE ULTIMATE RELATIONSHIP

Every relationship here on earth can mistakenly become an ultimate. Your relationship with your dad is not the ultimate source of love or happiness. Relationships deserve our time and attention, which is why we're opening this conversation about our dads. However, I pray it does not create a hypersensitivity to having the perfect dad-daughter relationship. If we ultimately go to our dads with our cravings, we will be looking to them for how they can benefit us, instead of connecting with who they are and receiving any benefits from that as a gift.

Tim Keller wrote a powerful little book unpacking Christ's parable about the prodigal son.[6] In it, he talks about the rebellious, younger son and the good, older son, and what they both represent. He says, "Jesus uses the younger and elder brothers to portray the two basic ways people try to find happiness and fulfillment: the way of moral conformity and the way of self-discovery."

He explains the younger son was "saying, essentially, that he wants his father's things but not his father." On the other hand, he says, "Elder brothers obey God to get things. They don't obey God to get God Himself—in order to resemble Him, love Him, know Him, and delight in Him."

Just like there are two kinds of sons, we can be two kinds of daughters. We can be the one who pushes for our own way. Or we can be the one who is good, knows what to do, and expects to earn a good life without the pure motivation of love and relationship. I have role-played each of these daughter types, both with my dad and with my God.

Before I was even a teenager, I had my prodigal moments. One night after an argument with my parents, I ran to my room, slid open my closet door, and reached for my empty (because homes-chooled), thrifted backpack. I flopped, frustrated, onto the floor, backpack lying on my lap. *Run away.* It felt logical. It would show them how they would miss and value me if I wasn't here. Show I was serious about what I was saying. Get their full attention. I never went through with the notion, but I don't think it was the last time I felt the urge.

Years later, I was a whole different girl and had a whole different relationship with my parents. Or so it seemed to me. God had turned our hearts toward each other. We had a peaceful, solid connection. But as an adult, I hit some challenging seasons of life that brought flashback feelings from my young teen years. I hardly understood why, but I began to wonder . . . what if I hadn't changed? What if I would have continually bucked the system, been a trial, rebelled, and resented my role as their daughter? What if I would have been a disgrace to my dad? Would I still have been valued? Would I still have been loved as his daughter?

For some reason I had to know this, and it made me want to grab that backpack and consider packing it again. I wouldn't actually do it. I loved Jesus and my parents, and I knew this wouldn't solve anything. But something inside me felt like I needed to test why I was loved.

It is unsettling to feel loved for how we benefit others. As good as it feels to benefit others, if our value is suspended by the rope of our performance, one can't help but be uneasy. Ropes like that can turn into threads before we know it.

It was one of the most confusing, odd seasons of my life. I had a great relationship with my dad, yet I still craved his approval and subconsciously tried to prove myself to him. I craved feeling truly seen and heard. I loved Jesus, yet wanted proof that He loved me for the sake of relationship, not just because I was good or sweet or did all the right things.

There were some things missing from my relationship with my dad when I was a young teen. Some unmet cravings left space for a few lies and disconnections. Even after our relationship improved, I had to face those lies about love and value that I believed before I knew how to behave better. This same dad I had felt disconnected from sat with his full-grown girl late into many nights, holding me as I faced these underlying lies. As I reckoned with what had wrongly motivated me, I began to taste of God and His unshakable, unconditional love like I never had before.

This odd season of my life made me realize something. We just want to be loved, don't we? And we desperately want to know it's a love that's directed toward us because of the goodness of the person loving us, not the goodness of what we do.

As Tim Keller says, "We aren't truly loved if we are loved for our goodness."[7] Whether we're little girls, good or bad women, rebellious teens, or capable adults, we all have a continual desire to be unconditionally loved, valued, known, and safe. And we especially want this with our dads. We crave it before we even know how to name it or understand what's going on.

It's why I as a daughter could do everything right and seemingly have a good relationship with my dad, but still sometimes feel confused about my inner longings and dissatisfactions. If

> HE ALSO JUST WANTS US AND LOVES US, WHETHER WE'VE BEEN GOOD OR BAD.

we don't know we're loved for the sake of relationship, we probably won't know how to give or receive love for the sake of relationship. Especially in our relationship with God.

The father in the prodigal story shows us that God wants to provide for us and give us an inheritance, and He wants us to honor and serve Him. But He also just wants us and loves us, whether we've been good or bad. He wants a relationship with us above all other things. When dads love their girls just for the sake of loving them, they are reflecting the heart of God. When they love selflessly, they emphasize that God's love is selfless. When dads love their girls without a personal agenda, they make the love of God more believable.

What if we, in turn, chose relationship as our chief motivation? What if we loved our dads for the sake of loving our dads? Not so we could get our "inheritance"—the feelings, experiences, and freedoms we want—but just entered into relationship because he's our dad and that matters. What if the first step in love was to come without an agenda to fix or even restore anything about our relationship? What if, before anything else, we came simply because of the value God places on our dad's position and person?

When we choose to love our dads because they are our dads, we make it believable that God is worth our love because He is God. When we love God for who He is, not what He gives us, we experience a satisfying, steady love. When we engage in relationship with Him without our own agenda, we begin to truly love Him.

When you think about the relational love of God, what comes to your mind? Does it ever feel a little unsafe? I think deep down we know: if we fully believed the relational love of God, all the performing would have to stop. All the ways we like to keep life comfortable would have to go. All the self-protecting would need to be replaced with fearlessness. All the ways we built our own identity would no longer hold a bearing on our decisions and actions.

I John 4:18 says, "Perfect love casts out fear." And sometimes fear is the very thing motivating our actions, so we're not sure if it's smart to let go of it and receive love in its place. Sometimes I think keeping a little bit of fearful performance around will guide me on the straight and narrow, because then I can use my own tools to be godly. Believing love somehow communicates that we would need to be entirely re-motivated by relationship. Which, maybe, is exactly what God intends to say when He names Himself "Father" and us "daughter."

ACTING
INTENTIONALLY

Are there any memories or emotions coming up for you as you ponder your relationship with your dad? What about your relationship with God? These may be positive or negative.

Either way, sometimes I find it helpful to make a small list of the things on my mind. Then I bring that list into the presence of God and ask Him my questions, give thanks for good gifts, and name my fears and emotions.

Sometimes I make these lists on a sticky note so I don't overthink what I'm writing or saying. You can just jot things down as they come, then throw it away after you've brought it to God.

One of my pastors told me recently that the biblical idea for "Father" often boils down to "source." Whatever you're bringing to Him, remember: He is the real source for what you crave.

ASK YOURSELF

- What craving do I have right now that I can ask Father God to fill?

- Do I relate most with the prodigal son or the hard-working son?

- What would change about my life this week if I believed I was loved because of who I am to God (a daughter) instead of what I do for God? What would change if I believed that today?

- What would change in my relationship or attitude toward my dad if I valued him for who he is instead of what he does or doesn't do for me?

NEVER BLAME YOUR DAD
FOR WHAT HE DID OR DIDN'T DO,
BUT STAND ON HIS SHOULDERS AND
plow new ground.

DAVE MILLER[1]

communication

LEARNING TO CONNECT WITH OUR DADS

Nelson Coblentz, the founder of Gospel Express Ministries, tells the moving story of the first time he hugged his dad and told him he loved him. He was twenty-five when those three words left his lips and met his father's ears. Then his dad, for the first time, responded with those same three, craved words.

I've heard him share the story a dozen different times in different churches, communities, and settings. I've also been privileged to see how God has completely restored their relationship. His father has accompanied him on a ministry trip to Africa and to numerous prisons, and he's stood with Nelson on stage many a night, praying at the start or end of a Gospel Express event. He is his son's supporter and encourager. Now, every time they leave each other or hang up the phone, they are intentional to use those three powerful words.

Nelson says, "It has to begin somewhere. And it starts when each new generation honors God's command to express love to one another."[2] He has lived enough life to know it's not always worth waiting for our dads to make the first move. Sometimes it's our turn to begin something.

It takes courage to do and say what wasn't done or said in the generation before us. Doing something new is always hard, but it's even harder to do something new in an old environment. Creating a new generation doing new things isn't as tricky as doing those new things *with* the older generation. Initiating conversation, connection, and restitution between separate generations is the stuff of unsuperficial honor. It calls individuals dealing with generation gaps to connect instead of live in reaction to each other.

The previous generation is not behind us. They have gone before us. When we reach out to connect between generations, we are not reaching toward someone stuck in the past, but toward someone who went before us and is coming around the circle to press the baton into our hands.

In a relay race, there is an intricate process of passing the baton between runners. The timing and technique must

> CREATING A NEW GENERATION DOING NEW THINGS ISN'T AS TRICKY AS DOING THOSE NEW THINGS WITH THE OLDER GENERATION.

be perfect so no time is lost. The forerunner must keep the baton steady and accessible and make sure the coming runner has a firm grip before letting go. It must be practiced and thought through.

Part of a father's role is to pass his baton into the hands of his children, freeing them to run their leg of the race. As the receivers of the baton, we need to be just as intentional about our role.

Do you know what happens when you drop the baton? I actually didn't, so I Googled it. Answers from an article by Kirsteen Farrance popped up bold and clear on my screen. It read, "If you drop the baton, you will be disqualified! If you run out of your lane during the baton pass, you will be disqualified! If you run out of the takeover zone without changing the baton, you will be disqualified! If you cross the finish line without the baton, you will be disqualified!"[3] If only she could've been more clear.

Reaching out to connect doesn't mean you're saying the generation before you ran well. It simply means you have to connect with the baton in their hand in order for you to run *your* race well. It may be time to extend our arms to connect with the forerunners through intentional communication.

CONNECTION THROUGH COMMUNICATION

I love communication, and I used to think I was good at it. But I found out I was actually good at *talking,* not *communicating.* I'm learning that communication isn't just about conversation. It's about connection.

The relationship I share with my sweet dad has been a greenhouse for growing in connection with someone who thinks differently than me. My dad and I work and play together. We live in the same house half the year and in the confines of a forty-foot bus the other half. With ministry, work, and events, we have many reasons between the two of us to make decisions and communicate.

As different as my dad and I are, we are alike in our determination to communicate, even if we don't always do it well. Neither of us is comfortable with a rug made lumpy from sweeping things underneath it. In our conversations, my dad has given me the impression that he would rather be connected to my heart than "win" in any given decision or discussion. He doesn't always know my heart's needs, and I don't always understand his, but he tries to focus more on connection than conclusion. Even when we can't agree on the next action or what is happening between us, we turn in for a hug and words of appreciation for each other.

If I'm uncertain of myself or what to do at the end of a conversation, he puts his hands on my shoulders and pumps confidence into my doubt with his words. When he does, I have the subtle feeling that he would trust me to be president of the world.

Picture our heavenly Father desiring connection with us like this. He will never stop pursuing communication with us so that we can know His heart for comradery and connection. We never have to be separated from His love. When we're confused or unable to get past ourselves, He desires to place His hands on our shoulders and pump heavenly perspective into our being.

At the same time, imagine His joy when we pursue communication with Him for the purpose of connection. Even our prayers change when they center around our desire to know Him and honor Him, no matter how much we don't understand His way of doing things. Connection-motivated communication can transform our understanding of how to have conversations with our dad and with our God.

OPENING THE CONVERSATION

Because our heavenly Father is always pursuing us, we sometimes think we should wait until our earthly fathers pursue us first too. But it can be hard for a dad to know how to connect with his girl when she's no longer little or thrilled with ice cream outings and bedtime tickles. Sometimes girls have to do some initiating to give their dads an opportunity to connect with them.

Some of the first hard conversations I had with my dad included honest confessions. Present day, there's rarely an opinion, situation, or crush I have that my dad doesn't know about. And I'm honored that I get to hear about his thoughts, decisions, frustrations, and joys as well. But as a young teen, starting conversations with my dad was awkward. Being honest about my failures, compromises, or temptations made me squirm. There were times I felt misunderstood by him. But I made the choice to endure the weird factor because it felt like connection and accountability was worth the risk.

Because my dad is an itinerant preacher, I grew up listening to the same sermons many times over. One of my favorites was Dad's sermon on restitution, probably because it included many first-hand stories. These stories were about Dad making peace with the people he had hurt and dishonored through his life before he knew Christ. His efforts for restitution included some honest talk with his parents—a life lesson he didn't know his own daughter would need.

My dad has taught me that whenever we experience transformation in our lives, it is an invitation to look at how we affected others before that transformation. We don't live alone. Our attitudes and actions are not confined within the safe walls we've built. My insecurities, control, peer-pressured decisions, texting flings, fudged rules, and anger were not just mine, they also affected my parents, who were giving of themselves to teach and train me.

I knew being half-hearted in my honesty or "praying about it" wasn't fully leading me to freedom. So I told them everything. The things I confessed didn't look terrible at the surface, but were still sinful in their motivation. They were attitudes, ways I had fudged the rules, weaseled my way out of their authority, and resented their voice in my life. There were compromises I was ashamed of and didn't want them to know about. Freedom from all of this didn't come until I owned my choices and was openly honest.

A friend of mine once told me her own story of restitution with her parents. She had recently been born again after years of living for what pleased herself. She had a conscience and knew right from wrong, but she didn't know Jesus personally, so her decisions were informed by her own will. After she came to know Him, the Holy Spirit and the Christian community around her began to disciple her. They helped guide her in lifestyle changes for the future, but also pointed her to look at the people she had affected in her past.

She started with her parents. Up to that point, she had not had safe, open channels of communication with them. The home she grew up in was good, but lacked heart-to-heart connection. The thought of being honest about her sin and the ways she had dishonored her parents was difficult.

She could have assumed they wouldn't fully appreciate her confession or understand her. She could have blamed her choices on how they failed her. But she didn't. She initiated a conversation of simple honesty.

This was hard and awkward. My friend wasn't used to confiding and being open with her parents, even under good circumstances. So talking about these dark places in her life was new and weird. She told her dad she was sorry for being loose with her purity when he had wanted to protect it. Graciously, she confessed the ways her choices undermined their role in her life. They hardly knew what to say to her, but it seemed her confession met them at a soft place. Instead of reacting to her words, they forgave her. Then they went a step further, recalling and confessing ways they had failed her as parents.

She told me how her whole house felt different after this conversation. Her vulnerability had softened the tension in her home. The process of learning to connect with her parents has continued to this day, but that one decision to confess and be open with her authorities has helped free her to walk away from the bondage of her past.

Many of you reading this book probably didn't live a life of immorality and empty pleasures like my friend did. But the combination of phones, movies, curiosity, and our sin nature leaves a lot of room for small things to happen that affect our lives in big ways. This can include things we've done or things done to us. Images and scenes we wish we hadn't seen. Things we wish we wouldn't have tried. Words we wish we hadn't read, typed, or said. An empty feeling we wish we wouldn't need to face.

Once I was chatting with a young girlfriend of mine on a Sunday afternoon. As we were talking, she began to open up about some choices she was ashamed of. She didn't know what to do with the darkness she felt from them.

I knew she had loving, understanding parents, so I asked her if she had ever told them about it. She said she had told her mom but was too scared to talk to her dad about it. It felt too vulnerable and hard.

I understood that all too well. I know how hard it was for me to be honest with my dad when I was young. Dads can feel so intimidating and otherworldly to the issues of a young girl. But somehow, even though she had shared it with her mom, there was still a lingering shame from her inability to talk about it with her dad.

This girl was innocent and young, living in a safe home environment—but that doesn't always keep us from experiencing sin that makes us feel dirty or doing things our conscience reacts to. I asked her if she thought it would be helpful to be honest with her dad. Something resolute in her said yes.

That same day, she talked to him. When I saw her again, I could relate to the look on her face. It spoke of the freedom that comes, and the trust that is built, when we are honest with our dads. Her dad had lovingly received her confession and prayed through the situation with her. It's a remarkable gift when girls have safe places to go, even if, at first, it's scary to go there.

"Confess your sins to one another and pray for one another, that you may be healed," says James 5:16. One of the biggest barriers to walking in freedom is keeping things hidden. With our dads we often think, *He won't understand me. He'll get angry when he finds out. Just confess it to God and pretend it never happened. What he doesn't know won't hurt him.* However, simple, honest confession will always be one of the greatest allies for living healed and healthy in relationships.

COMMUNICATING WITH THE LIGHTS ON

It is difficult enough to start the conversation. But starting a dialogue doesn't promise that communication will go smoothly. Have you ever left a conversation feeling confused or unsettled? Maybe you entered it to clarify something, understand someone, find resolve, or choose a next step. Instead, you became more confused, you felt misunderstood, you found reactions instead of resolutions, and you had no idea what the next step should be.

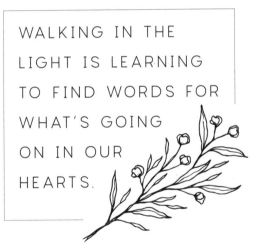

WALKING IN THE LIGHT IS LEARNING TO FIND WORDS FOR WHAT'S GOING ON IN OUR HEARTS.

Sometimes conversations can feel like we're fumbling around in a dark room, trying to make sense of things without the lights on.

First John 1 draws a parallel between truth and light. I like that. Truth has the effect of light in our lives. It gives us the ability to see things as they actually are, instead of feeling around a dim room and trying to make sense of shadows and illusions. John says that if we walk in the light, we have fellowship with God and each other. In other words, we're able to connect and enjoy a relationship with each other. Part of walking in the light is learning to find words for what's going on in our hearts and being willing to bring those things into the light, even if we don't understand them yet.

Ashley is a friend of mine who doubles as a mentor. I admire the way she lives. I also admire her relationship with her dad. Years ago, I sent out a questionnaire about father-daughter relationships to a few of my friends, because I was curious about others' stories. I took note of Ashley's response. She said:

> Growing up, I never felt very close to my dad. I never shared with him the desires of my heart, or openly shared the details of my day with him. In my teen years, I felt very alone and believed the lie that Dad never understood me or had my good in mind. There was a wall. . . . Every discussion ended in an argument, and I would walk away feeling hurt, and he felt disrespected.
>
> The biggest turnaround for me was at age twenty. I realized that my expectations for security, fulfillment, and praise were misplaced. Instead of looking to the Lord to meet the desires of my heart, I had been looking to my dad. This had brought a lot of disappointment.
>
> So when I opened up about this to my dad, a wall came down. I poured out all the disappointment, the hurt, and the wounded heart that I was carrying. I confessed secret sins and just became transparent. It was a true transformation, but still a work-in-progress. Now there is nothing in my life that needs to be hidden from him. I can trust him with my heart. I feel very protected, appreciated, and loved.

Her story draws out some common issues we girls can face with our dads. She talked about confessing hidden sins, as we've already discussed. But she also talked about another type of honesty. The kind that is expressed not through confession, but through exposing what's in our hearts. Ashley talked about expectations, disappointments, desires, and walls—not to blame her dad, but to bring them into the light.

Ashley reminds us of this powerful truth: when we look to God first, being honest becomes about connecting with our dads by exposing any walls or lies that would break that connection. She also named a few of the reasons we don't often share honestly with our dads. One being that we're afraid they won't understand us.

It's easy for a father and daughter to misunderstand each other because we're women and they're men. We're young, and they may seem ancient. We may have a different personality than our dad. All of this makes for easy miscommunication.

Far too often, we are happy to prove ourselves right by naming our dad as the bad guy—he doesn't get us, he wouldn't understand, he doesn't have good in mind for us. There are times our dads truly don't understand us or know how to relate to us. But this is where honesty helps.

When we have honest conversations with our dads, let's do it to set them up for success instead of failure. Let's assume they have good in mind, instead of making them the automatic bad guys. I'm the first to admit I tend to shift blame to my dad when we aren't communicating well. I forget that I, too, could be misunderstanding him. Sometimes sharing what we desire from our dad, being honest about how we feel, or talking about where we're at, can help him better understand how to relate to us. This can give him an opportunity to help us understand him as well.

Communicating from our hearts could mean saying things like:

"That comes across like you care less about me and more about what other people think."

"It would mean a lot to me if we could make this a priority."

"I need to feel like you trust me in this situation."

"I would love to be able to have more time with you."

"When you did that, this is what I felt . . ."

"I have a hard time feeling your love when you . . ."

When we communicate what's on our hearts, it's not so we can control our dads and get them to do what we want. It's not because we expect them to meet all our needs or desires. We're not saying it's their fault that we feel the way we do. We're simply being honest about what's going on for us in our relationship, and giving them permission to do the same. These efforts to bring what's inside into the light can help us stay focused on connection.

This doesn't mean you have to continually talk with your dad about everything you're dealing with. It means recognizing when you are blocking connection with him and seeking a way to bridge that broken connection.

THE REAL ISSUE

In order to bridge broken connections, we often have to peel back surface issues to see the real issue. As a young teen, I was quick to communicate about the issues I thought I saw clearly, but I wasn't communicating what was causing these issues.

I remember when I thought my parents' clothing standards were the one thing between me and happiness. I felt like their boundaries would be the brutal death of me.

At that age, I didn't know how to communicate what was really going on. All I knew was what I wanted. I wanted to wear that blue shirt that my parents felt was too skimpy. When they would caution or forbid what I wanted, I would say, "You're just being so picky," and tell them, "So-and-so does this all the time." I wondered why it was so wrong. I thought the problem was my dad's ideas. And the solution? His surrender.

This made connection almost impossible. The way I presented what I wanted left him with one option: let me do what I want or lose the right to connect with me. And sometimes, he would let me do what I wanted because he wanted peace and connection.

But if I would have communicated the real issue beneath the surface issue, I would have been saying, "Dad, I don't feel like I'm beautiful or worth accepting, and I want to be." If I had been honest, it wasn't just the clothes. It was a craving to be seen as valuable and beautiful. I assumed that being accepted by my friends or having boys think I was pretty would solve my problem. In my head, I could have told you this was a lie. But my proving, pushing, and pulling showed that I was trying to medicate an illness I didn't understand.

Thankfully, my dad is a remarkable dad, so he began to understand the motivations behind my reaction before I knew how to express them. He started using more affirming words about my person and my beauty. Instead of merely correcting me when I pushed for something he didn't agree with, he began to ask me why I wanted to do it. Then he spoke affirmation that helped diffuse the questions I had about my worth.

Like the steady drip of a faucet, this shift filled up the emptiness in our relationship. It was like watching Malachi 4:6 come to life. God was creating a mutual motion inside each of us, turning our hearts toward each other.

If your dad never recognizes the real issue behind your reactions, see if communicating from your heart helps him understand. Had I simply begun to talk about my desire to be beautiful and express that beauty, I think my conversations with my dad would have become clearer. Practice sharing the desires and questions of your heart with your dad. It may help you both get to the real issue you're dealing with.

When I was a young adult, my dad and I had a whole different set of things to deal with. My family's ministry presents a unique lifestyle for all involved. And this ministry is also my job.

Family, ministry, and work being mixed all together can create challenges and blessings. When my dad and I made schedules or plans, the conversations were often tense, topped off with an uncanny ability to misunderstand each other.

I remember a season when I felt tired and frustrated with my ministry and work schedule. When I voiced this to my dad, he assured me he was trying to schedule in a way that would be healthy for the whole family. He also freed me to quit traveling if that is what I felt was best. For some reason, these answers didn't fix my problem.

I started to ask myself what exactly I was seeking from these conversations. I wanted to be a part of what was going on with my family. So why, at the same time, did I resent what was included in the package?

It took me a while to understand what the real issue was. Underneath my reactions were lies that said my value was defined by what I contributed. Had I been honest, instead of saying, "Can we please travel less?" I would have said, "I need to know my value to you and God is not defined by how I contribute to this work."

Once I understood this, I was able to explain to my dad *why* I felt so exhausted and reactionary about our schedule. These lies, labels, and perceptions of myself were fueling my tiredness. Once I voiced the real issue behind my reactions to Dad, he instinctively became more gentle in our conversations. The last thing he wanted was for his girl to believe lies because of our family lifestyle. I remember crying on his shoulder often as he helped me walk through years of subtle performance I didn't understand and couldn't put into words. I'm crying now as I write, remembering the shift in our conversations when we stopped blaming things that were only the surface results of the real issue.

Ideally, dads will notice the real issues behind the reactions of their daughters. But just like we want them to give us grace and understanding, we need to give it to them too. Dads need help to understand us. Most times, they welcome it. It's helpful when we understand ourselves so we can communicate our real needs to them. Then there is potential for authentic connection.

CREATING A SAFE RELATIONSHIP

When we communicate, we cannot control what our dads will do. If they don't know how to respond, it is not our job to coerce them into responding like we think they should.

If you find there isn't safety in your relationship with your dad, ask trusted advisors (probably someone other than your high school BFF) how to create needed boundaries in order to maintain honor for your dad, without putting yourself in a victimized situation.

Notice I said boundaries, not walls. We humans automatically sense when something or someone isn't safe. Especially as children. Instinctively, we do what it takes to protect ourselves. The problem is, without the transformation of the Holy Spirit, our protection skills consist of things like anger, bitterness, shutting down, pretending we don't care, acting like we don't have the same needs as other people, overachieving, mouthing off, refusing to talk, or convincing ourselves and others that we're fine.

I believe God wants your heart to be safe. But He wants the right kind of safety. The kind that protects you from lies that can damage your eternal soul. Not the kind that protects you from people He wants you to connect with, or even from the hard circumstances that cause growth in your life.

The Bible uses a shield to describe faith, like it's our protection. Our faith has to do with what we believe about God, which defines what we believe about ourselves and others. Usually the most unsafe relationships happen when people have their shields down and their walls up. When we put down our faith—a belief system rooted in truth—by allowing lies in and acting from them, we're setting ourselves up for unhealthy communication. As the stories above illustrate, I do this all the time. But those stories are also a testimony to the natural safety that comes when the shield of faith is present.

Having a faith rooted in truth will help us to know how to have both freedom and boundaries in our relationships. If you have tried communicating from your heart and your dad is still unable to have respectful conversations, ask God how you can wisely create boundaries in your relationship.

WHEN WE KNOW THE TRUTH OF OUR VALUE IN CHRIST, WE WILL CREATE BOUNDARIES THAT LINE UP WITH THE TRUTH.

All relationships need boundaries, spoken or unspoken, in order for both individuals to thrive within them. A boundary draws a line to keep us from cycles of misuse, disrespect, or burnout in our relationships. But these lines should follow truth. When we know the truth of our value in Christ, we will create boundaries that line up with the truth. If we're believing lies, boundaries may not take care of the real issues in our hearts. They cannot ultimately lead us to truth or freedom—boundaries should be a result of truth and freedom.

When we communicate honestly about what's in our hearts, we often set ourselves up for more naturally healthy boundaries. I talked about two different seasons of my life when there were clear communication issues. Understanding the lies beneath my reactions, and voicing them honestly, helped my dad and me understand what kind of boundaries we needed to have in those areas of our lives. Sometimes we needed to have clear conversations about boundaries. Other times they simply came as a result of understanding each other.

After my dad and I had a better heart connection, clothing choices were almost never an issue between us. We were both walking in clearer truth and understanding each other better, and this resulted in mutual trust. This helped us understand the boundary of both staying within our roles as I became an adult. Dad was there to impart values and standards that promote biblical beauty, and I was free to make personal choices within those values and standards.

These days, our communication about clothing usually only takes place if I ask Dad's opinion on something. I genuinely want to know if something I'm wearing distracts from the gospel that directs my life. I'll ask him things like, "Dad, is this shirt just too much?" or "Is this dress too tight?" Most times, he's a big fan of what I'm wearing and often tells me I'm beautiful.

I'm grateful I have someone helping me understand how to walk in honor with my own body. And if I choose to do something that isn't Dad's preference, we talk about it. We no longer need to overthink or stress about this subject because we have built mutual trust, understanding, and boundaries.

When it comes to our ministry schedule, once we dealt with the lies causing the misunderstandings and reactions in our conversation, we were able to address practical scheduling issues in the light. These honest conversations also helped us understand our own needed boundaries within our ministry relationship. As I brought the real issue, I was saying, "If I give you this much access to my schedule, I need to be able to trust I will not be pushed beyond my capacity on a regular basis."

And my dad's honesty helped me understand his boundaries as well. He was saying, "If you, as an adult, are committed to this ministry, I need to know if you can understand and thrive within the responsibilities involved." We rarely have conflict in this area anymore because we both understand each other's needs and boundaries. Dad is careful to prioritize what's important to me and schedule our travels with intentional rest in mind. And I understand and thrive within my responsibilities.

A boundary may include releasing yourself from the pressure to communicate with your dad the way you'd want to. If he is unable to engage in healthy conversation, it may be a season to simply accept this. This doesn't make you exempt from showing him honor or give you permission to close your heart to his potential for growth. But it may mean you are in a season of letting go of desires, even for good things like connection with your dad. Sometimes accepting the status of our current relationship helps us know better what to do next. Sometimes it helps us realize the subtle ways we were trying to control the relationship, instead of simply being faithful in it. Maybe saying, "I don't know how to communicate with my dad right now," and sitting in this discomfort is exactly what will help you understand why this is the case.

Relationships are a funny thing. Sometimes the best thing we can do is press in deeper toward the person we're in a relationship with. Other times, creating honorable distance facilitates the work of God in each of our lives. But always, no matter what relational steps we're taking, let us be in truth, not lies; in love, not fear; and in light, not darkness.

ACTING
INTENTIONALLY

I'm learning if a conversation surrounding a certain topic continually causes tension, the real issue probably isn't being addressed. Let this be a checkpoint. When things aren't resolving well, ask God to bring you revelation. Are there labels on yourself or your dad that you're reacting to? Are there lies, filters, or pain causing the breakdown? Is there broken trust? How might God want to rebuild that trust, speak truth to lies, rip off labels, and clean out filters?

I remember Ashley once told me what she chooses to do when she and her dad misunderstand each other: "Instead of pulling away from my dad, I choose to keep pursuing him, keep opening up to him, and keep talking so we can understand each other."

ASK YOURSELF

- What can I learn from the way my dad and his generation ran their race?

- What words or conversations do I need to share or have with my dad?

- Is there anything breaking the connection between my dad and me right now?

- Are there any boundaries that would make my relationship with my dad healthier?

- What lies might I be believing that keep me from setting up these boundaries?

THE GOODNESS OF GOD
IS INFINITELY MORE

wonderful

THAN WE WILL
EVER BE
ABLE TO
COMPREHEND.

A. W. TOZER[1]

goodness

HOW DELIGHT AND DISCIPLINE
AFFECT OUR SOULS

We sat on bleachers in the prison gymnasium, praying. It was my mom, two female chaplains, and myself, asking God for His presence to be with us in this place. Meanwhile, my dad and brothers set up our sound system before the female inmates arrived. They were doing their job in their usual efficient, professional way when a few glitches started to show up.

Normally we play our soundtracks from an iPad, which we couldn't bring into this institution. The staff promised us they had plenty of little boomboxes around that we could use instead. They brought one out, and I watched, between prayers, as they discovered it wouldn't do the job. So they pulled another one from somewhere in the institution. Same story.

Finally, they brought out a third option. I smiled when I saw it, my memory transporting me to the aisle of an unorganized Walmart in North Carolina.

I was probably around ten years old when my parents told me I was allowed to pick out my own CD player as a birthday present. Imagine ten-year-old Deborah, cheeks a little chubby and hair slicked back into a tight ponytail, standing in the electronics aisle as her dreams were coming true. I landed on the model I liked most. There were two color options. One was silver with blue speakers and accents, while the other was accented in orange.

I stressed over the choice like it would change the course of my future forever. But eventually it became clear: an orange boombox would give me the cool card of the century. My dad picked up the big box with the orange CD player, and we floated home.

I cleared a small stand in my room as my dad opened the box on the floor next to me. Then the deflating moment happened. The box with the picture of the orange boombox contained a blue one instead. I was beyond disappointed. It was too late to go back and replace it that night. If I truly wanted an orange boombox, I would have to wait until another day when we had time to go back to Walmart. I couldn't test out my VeggieTales CD or have my first live concert with Twila Paris and a hand-held ice cream scoop. I went to bed that night watching my empty stand and a box full of the wrong content.

The next morning, I opened my eyes and they fell on that same stand. But instead of an empty spot, there sat a glistening silver CD player with orange speaker cages. Was I dreaming?

I ran out to the kitchen and asked my mom for an explanation. She smiled wide. Dad woke up extra early that morning, she told me. He drove twenty-five minutes to our nearest Walmart and exchanged the CD player, double-checking the box content before he left the store. He returned home, unpacked the box, and set up the player before he left for work that morning. "He knew how disappointed you were last night," she said. "So he wanted to surprise you."

The boombox that finally worked for our sound system at the women's prison was the exact model as that first boombox I got for my birthday. Only, it was the blue one. I knew what I would share with the ladies that night.

When my turn came to introduce a song during our service, I pointed to the CD player behind me on the stage, and I told them the story. There were "awws" and tears instantly.

Inmates often tell painful stories about their fathers. Many never even knew their biological dad. Others were abused, yelled at, or taught the tough life of drugs and fending for themselves. So when

I told them about a Father God who is constant, interested in the details of their lives, and longs to give them good gifts, well, the chaplains ran for TP to pass around as tissues.

Then, my dad started crying. My brother stood up to sing his solo, and I sat down on a stool on the stage and broke down. I had been sick for the last twenty-four hours, and the past few months had been some of the most difficult of my life. So the reminder of the Father's love touched me as personally as it did these women. My brother sang, and the rest of us sobbed.

As I ponder these memories now, I realize it wasn't getting the orange CD player that made me break down on stage more than a decade later. It was the story of the goodness of my dad, and the memories of how this connected me to him. But as I look back on my childhood relationship with my dad, I can see that my safety, delight, and connection with him was not created just from moments like the orange boombox, but also from moments after I had been punished and corrected by him.

WHEN DISCIPLINE IS THE GIFT

The love and goodness of our dads knit our hearts to them. But in order for them to be good dads, they also need to correct and train us to be women of character, knowing right from wrong. Respect, safety, and trust are built not just through good gifts, but also through the gift of good discipline.

> RESPECT, SAFETY, AND TRUST ARE BUILT NOT JUST THROUGH GOOD GIFTS, BUT ALSO THROUGH THE GIFT OF GOOD DISCIPLINE.

I have a memory of my dad disciplining me when I was about four years old. I can't recall what I had done wrong anymore, just the tearful moment after the punishment.

This memory is one of the most safe, loving memories

I have from my early childhood. You would think that correction, discipline, and training would drive a child away from her parent. But when motivated out of love instead of anger, it does just the opposite. After the loving, firm punishment, the only place I wanted to be was in his arms. And he welcomed me there. He rocked and held me as I cried.

There was no condemnation, distance, or shame from this punishment. I felt guilt first, but that was immediately followed by feeling clean, safe, and close to my dad. After I was done crying, he wiped my tears, reaffirmed his love for me, and we exchanged smiles and kisses.

When the Bible describes the goodness of God, it uses the idea of a father to tell the story. A Father who desires to give good gifts to His children. Often when we hear about the goodness of God, it's on a Facebook post alongside someone's wedding day photos or the birth of a child. These are stories like the boombox, when God provides something beautiful and specific to the desires of our hearts. But the goodness of God has little to do with good circumstances. Just like a good dad isn't measured by how much he spoils his kids, but rather by how he both disciplines and delights in his kids.

> "It is for discipline that you have to endure. God is treating you as sons. For what son is there whom his father does not discipline? If you are left without discipline, in which all have participated, then you are illegitimate children and not sons. Besides this, we have had earthly fathers who disciplined us and we respected them. Shall we not much more be subject to the Father of spirits and live? For they disciplined us for a short time as it seemed best to them, but he disciplines us for our good, that we may share his holiness. For the moment all discipline seems painful rather than pleasant, but later it yields the peaceful fruit of righteousness to those who have been trained by it" (Hebrews 12:7–11).

These verses unpack something remarkable about the nature of God: the chastening, waiting, and correction of the Father is always for our life. His correction and biblical boundaries teach us to enter into the fear of God and the safety of His lap. When we experience Christ and walk with Him, we have the privilege of feeling clean, close, and safe, even when we've been corrected by Him. Because these are the gentle, wise ways of Father God, designed to knit our hearts to Him

It was in some of my hardest, darkest days that I began to understand that it is *God* who is good, not just His gifts and blessings. Being disciplined did not feel good to me. But because I knew my dad was good, I could turn around to him, cry the needed tears, and connect even more deeply with the safety of his presence.

This one truth, that God is a good Father, is something I return to even more frequently than I return binge purchases from T.J. Maxx (you don't want to know how often). I need continual reminders that He's interested in the personal desires of my heart. He is not full of shame or distance when He corrects. He is full of truth and grace. He is only ever interested in our good, which means He cannot leave us without healthy correction and training. Whether we're receiving gifts or being trained, remember, in both we are given access to be brought nearer to Father God.

Hebrews 5:8 says that even Jesus had to learn through suffering: "Although he was a son, he learned obedience through what he suffered." I'm in awe of this idea. Our perfect Jesus was willing to learn, even though He hadn't done anything wrong. So remember, trials don't necessarily mean we've done something wrong either. Sometimes they are simply there to teach us obedience, just as Jesus was taught.

Oswald Chambers said, "Faith must be tested, because it can be turned into a personal possession only through conflict."[2] When our faith is set in Christ, times of testing, discipline, and questions can turn what we *know* about the goodness of God into personally *experiencing* the goodness of God.

EXPERIENCING THE GOODNESS OF GOD

Psalm 34:8 says, *"Taste* and *see* that the LORD is good!" God desires that we both *taste* of His goodness, and *see* the goodness of the way

He does things. This moves us past knowing things about Him and into experiencing Him personally.

If I told you that Talenti's® salted caramel gelato tastes good—like, *really* good—you'd probably believe me. If I set some in front of you, you'd see the silky-smooth cream softening in your small glass dish, and you'd probably be even more convinced. But if you'd never tasted it, just looked at it and acknowledged how good it would probably be, then how solid would your belief be?

If someone else came along, looked at you and then the bowl of glorious gelato, and said, "You do not want to eat that! Last time I had it, I was sick for three days." Suddenly, even if you said you believed me, you would start to question if it was worth trying.

But if you had already tasted this goodness, and experienced delicious flavors without any bad side effects, no one could tell you differently. You would have to conclude that the person who got sick probably had a bigger issue, like lactose intolerance or a sugar sensitivity. Or maybe they had an off-brand version with shady ingredients. In any case, you'd question their experience first, not the gelato. When we experience something, we're no longer merely believing something about it, we are personally affected by it.

> WHEN WE EXPERIENCE HIM, WE BEGIN TO BECOME LIKE HIM.

First Peter 2:2–3 says, "Like newborn infants, long for the pure spiritual milk, that by it you may grow up into salvation—if indeed you have *tasted that the Lord is good.*" God wants us to taste of Him firsthand. It's part of how we "grow up" as His girls, forming our beliefs around who He is.

When we experience Him, we begin to become like Him, loving what He loves and doing as He does, just like when we were little girls, naturally absorbing what our dads love and do.

As a child, I remember wanting to do what I saw my dad doing. One clear memory of my imitation happened at McDonald's, of all places.

Our local McDonald's was not one of those that tried to improve its image by looking more modern and adding salads to the menu. It was classic, with Ronald McDonald waving out front next to the germ-infested playground, and Big Macs and McNuggets gracing the old menu. But in my young mind, it was still exciting to go.

I wasn't old enough to order by myself, so I conveyed my desired Happy Meal to my dad, and he told the lady with the navy visor. A soda must have been included in the Happy Meal because I was allowed to have one, which was out of the ordinary. The soda machine was too high for my reach, so Dad held my cup and asked what I wanted to drink.

"Diet Coke," I told him.

He questioned me, of course. Surely, this wasn't actually what his scrawny little girl wanted. He was probably thinking, *Sprite, Mountain Dew, Hi-C, anything but a diet soda.* But I insisted. I could tell he almost felt bad to let me have it, but maybe he finally caught my underlying motive. I wanted Diet Coke because I knew it's what he liked. I had never tried it before, so I had no idea if I would like it. I just wanted to do what I saw my dad doing.

In John 5:19, Jesus said He only did what He saw the Father doing. What a statement. Everything we know about our loving Jesus was Him living out what He watched His Father do.

We often do what we see our fathers do, even if we're unaware of it, because we're in their presence, watching them. We're forming beliefs around what we've experienced by being near to them.

Because my dad is an itinerant preacher, many people know about him. They know what he believes and what he stands for in a broad sense. But when I listen to my dad's sermons, I hear them differently than most people. I know not just what he stands for, but also how he thinks. I know the background of the stories he shares and the intentions of why he says what he does. I see the way he lives what he's talking about. I experience him in a whole different way than the people who are simply listening to him from a distance. I have close access to him. I get to sit on his lap, hear his favorite jokes a dozen times over, and watch the way he lives. Because I have experienced him up close, I not only know what he's like, I also become a little bit like him.

Just by being around our dads we learn how they think. We take on their gestures and priorities. We pick up on their dreams and ideas. Our belief systems become formed by the way we see them live, whether it is good or bad. Some of us have grown up, tasted diet sodas, and realized we didn't like them after all. But it probably took some discovery, because the good and bad of our dads' beliefs knit their way into the formation of our own from infancy.

In this same way, when we begin to taste and see who our Father God is, we start acting like Him. We are close. Near. We eat from the table of His household. So we crave more of what is set on the table there. We take on His ways of thinking, and our belief system begins to be transformed. We start doing what we see Him doing, because we've experienced the goodness of being near Him.

The goodness of God includes gifts and blessings that are as personal as orange speakers instead of blue. He cares about the desires of our hearts. He'd like to know which soda we truly want. But the goodness of God is also the very thing that leads us to repentance, awe, and obedience. Paul says in Romans 2:4, "The goodness of God leads you to repentance" (NKJV). The goal of both His delight and His discipline is to bring us near to Himself so we can experience Him personally.

The way we experience our dads' delight and discipline forms our belief system. And the way we experience God's delight and discipline *transforms* our belief system. All this takes place on the inside, in what the Bible often refers to as our soul.

CONDUCTING OUR SOULS

Our belief systems are developed in our souls. Part of our role as adults is managing our souls. God is the owner. We have been bought with a price.[3] But He gives us the privilege of being stewards of our souls. It is His truth that transforms us. His voice that leads us. But it is our choice to come into agreement with Him that lets this happen. It takes our "yes" to His pursuit that allows Him to transform our souls.

God is so relational, He allowed our mental, emotional, and physical development to be dependent on people, giving us a picture of our dependence on Him. He gave our parents a lot of power in our lives. Our dads are given a massive responsibility with the words they speak to us, the tone they say them in, the love they give or withhold, and the way they teach and train us. All these things affect our soul and what we believe about ourselves, others, and God.

Each soul is made up of mind, will, and emotions. It's as though we're an orchestra, multifaceted and dynamic, and we need a director to engage with every instrument in us. We need a cue for the violins, the percussion, the brass, the cellos. We need someone to activate our conscience, engage with our emotions, ignite our imaginations, train our will, create positive memories, and comfort us in the negative ones.

When we were children, our parents were the conductors for our souls. But no parents, no matter how saintly, will have conducted the music in their home perfectly. It's a good thing, too, because the ultimate conductor of our souls should be the Spirit of God. The way our parents engage with us is just a picture of what it's like to allow someone bigger than us to conduct our souls.

Every one of us will have a section in our orchestra that has to work harder than the others. One reason for this is our personality and natural strengths and weaknesses. What comes naturally to one does not to another. I've heard parents say it all the time: what works for one child doesn't for the next. What hurt you may not have hurt your sibling. How you perceived and experienced your dad may be different than someone raised in the same house, because you had a different way of thinking and understanding. Our personalities affect the natural ways we perceive others and what parts of our soul may need some intentional work.

But beyond personality, the soul is affected by how we were raised by our dads. It's also affected by our moms, friends, teachers, extended family, tragedies, siblings, and so on. Our dads are simply one aspect of what affects our souls.

When we recognize the parts of ourselves that haven't been trained or tuned up much, let it be an invitation for more of Christ, not an opportunity to blame our dads for what they didn't do. It's okay if each section wasn't trained well. We all need to take responsibility for our own lives as we grow into adulthood. Even if people failed to help us develop to the best of our ability, we aren't ever stuck there or defined by that. When we take responsibility for what we believe, we give God the opportunity to transform our negative experiences into the places we experience the goodness of God.

With that in mind, it is helpful to honestly evaluate how we were raised and what elements of our souls have not been engaged with as they could have been. Many of our dads got a lot of it right, but none of them got it all right. You know what's funny about that? It's just as important for Jesus to enter into the places they got it right as the places they got it wrong. If we let our dads' love replace God's love instead of lead us to His love, we're still disconnected from Him. If we let our good upbringing define our identity, instead of lead us to our identity in Christ, we're still self-sufficient.

ALL THE GOOD OUR DADS BRING US IS AN INVITATION TO EXPERIENCE EVEN MORE OF THE SAME WITH GOD, NOT TO TAKE HIS PLACE.

I've done that plenty of times. I've felt loved and confident because I could trust my upbringing or the status of my last name, instead of feeling loved and confident because I've been brought into the house of God and given a new name. I've felt safe because of my relationship with my dad, but couldn't feel safe to trust God without it. All the good our dads bring us is an invitation to experience even more of the same with God, not to take His place. And all of the bad our dads bring us is an invitation to experience something different and better from God, not to define who He is.

WHAT WAS VALUED IN YOUR HOME?

The values within the homes we were raised in aren't automatically good just because that's the way we were brought up.

What was valued in your home? Was your soul shut down, or was it engaged and trained? Was one part of your soul elevated over the other? Perhaps your will was trained, but you were never engaged with emotionally. Maybe your intellect was educated, but your mind never perceived kind words and interactions from your dad. Was your home ruled by emotions, or were emotions used for healthy connection, healing, and growing?

As you dive deeper into these questions, I hope you can celebrate where you connected with your dad and grieve and surrender where you didn't. I hope these questions allow space to experience the goodness of God like you haven't dared to before.

HOW DID YOUR DAD ENGAGE
WITH YOUR MIND?

Dr. Caroline Leaf, a Christian cognitive neuroscientist, says that our minds and brains are not the same thing, but separate things that work together. Our brains are physical, but as Dr. Leaf says, the mind is "this wonderful spiritual, non-physical part of you that is so powerful that every time that you think and feel and choose, you're actually changing something about how you . . . function."[4] Our mind allows us to think and uniquely perceive the world around us.

How did you perceive your dad while growing up? Did he seem close, fun, or welcoming? Were you afraid of him or drawn to him? Did you perceive him to be safe? As you watched and took subconscious notes on what he loved, how he talked, and what he praised, what did you perceive about who God was and who you were?

Did it seem like your dad had a pure mind you could trust? Or did his demeanor cause you to distrust him?

When dads deeply delight in their girls, their daughters' minds perceive that they are created with value, worth, and purpose.

When dads themselves have pure minds, their daughters can feel this loyalty and trustworthiness. This helps girls perceive that people, and men especially, can be trusted. When their dads protect and train them, girls' minds perceive they are valuable. When dads plant truth in their daughters' minds, they grow life inside them.

God is in the constant business of renewing our minds. No matter how our dads engaged with our minds, and no matter how we saw them use their own minds, we can choose to take our thoughts captive to the obedience of Christ (2 Corinthians 10:5).

HOW DID YOUR DAD ENGAGE WITH YOUR WILL?

Through our parents, we learn what it's like for our will to be trained by someone who cares for us. Our will helps us make choices. Through our will we choose between right and wrong. We choose who's in charge. Our will can be trained to do the right thing and be responsible, even when we don't feel like it or it's inconvenient or hard.

Were you trained in self-control, diligence, and obedience? Or were you left to train yourself in many ways?

Were you trained by a certain set of rules, but never taught to develop personal boundaries and convictions? Were you ever taught why you do what you do? Were you left to be trained by the environment of a certain church or culture? Was your will (doing the "right" thing) elevated so highly in your home that you lost touch with your emotions or weren't taught to think?

When dads train their daughters' wills, their daughters learn to become life-giving, responsible adults. When they say things like, "What you did was wrong," without implying, "There is something wrong with who you are," they help create a healthy consciousness of sin and consequences.

Philippians 2:13 says, "It is God who works in you both to *will* and to *do* for His good pleasure" (NKJV). Whatever your story is, submitting your will to the leadership of Jesus Christ allows Him to be Himself in you.

HOW DID YOUR DAD ENGAGE WITH YOUR EMOTIONS?

Emotions are an interesting subject. Sometimes it almost seems like life would be easier without them. We stuff them down or shut them off when they're too painful, uncomfortable, or confusing. But then we run into another issue: this shutting down also shuts us off from connecting with people and feeling emotions like love and joy the way we want to.

Or maybe we do the opposite with our emotions—we don't stuff them, but we let them overwhelm us or control our relationships.

I've heard it said that unhealthy emotions are a bit like the check-engine light in your car. They can give us alert signals that something may be wrong. These alert signals don't mean what you're feeling is accurate or true, it's just signaling that what you're believing in your heart may be a lie.

Even if we know the truth in our heads, what we feel gives us a signal for what we believe at a core level. When our intellect knows one thing but our heart believes another, we will be in continual battle within ourselves. James 1 refers to this as being "double-minded," which causes us to be unstable and driven with the wind. I know that instability all too well.

For years I assumed that if my emotions didn't align with the truth, I needed to ignore what I was feeling. I thought I had to stuff down whatever didn't agree with the truth, take a deep breath, and trudge forward, exhausted. That's kind of like sitting in your car telling yourself how well it's running when it's actually broken down beside the road. Instead of doing that, it may be smart to look into the issue that caused your car to break down in the first place. I once heard Dennis Rainey, host of FamilyLife Today® say, "In many homes, emotions are told to be suppressed instead of expressed or explored."[5]

I've heard some girls say they were told to suppress any emotion at all in their homes. As if emotions were considered unspiritual. Others have said positive emotions were permitted, but expressing any kind of sadness, tears, or disappointment was not. Some were allowed to use their emotions to control their environment. Yet others have expressed that negative emotion was most of what they felt at home—anger, frustration, sadness, tension—and so they felt like they needed to be the ones to ease the tension and make everything okay and happy.

When dads welcome the emotions of their daughters and teach them how to use them for connecting and understanding, instead of control and manipulation, they equip their girls for the variety of sorrows and joys life brings. When they allow their own emotions to be expressed to their daughter, they invite her to connect beyond a surface level. When girls see emotions of delight, joy, and compassion on their dads' faces, it teaches them how to engage with the world around them in healthy ways.

Dennis Rainey lists some of the emotions the Bible says God Himself experiences: gladness, grief, delight, love, pleasure, regret, longing, and hurt, to name a few. There will be parts of Him, and us, we will miss if we don't enter into the emotion of God and if we don't encounter the expression of the Father toward our lives. We should not be led by our emotions, but we can let our emotions lead us to God.

No matter how our dads did or didn't connect with us emotionally, we always have the opportunity to bring emotion under the leadership of the Holy Spirit, learning about Jesus, who gives rest to our souls.

A NEW CONDUCTOR

A dad is not only meant to implant truth in your mind through his demeanor and words, he is also meant to train your will. A dad is not only meant to train your will, he is also meant to engage with you emotionally. Your dad was meant to be present with you so you could experience him personally.

In the same way, God doesn't want you to only know Him with your mind, or only with your will, or only with your emotions, or only through certain experiences you've had with Him. He wants to connect with you in each of these ways as you allow the Holy Spirit to be the ruler of your soul and the definer of your experiences. Spirituality is not elevating one part of your soul over the other. Spirituality is bringing your experiences and each aspect of your soul under the leadership of the Holy Spirit.

We need a good Father. We need someone to show us what it takes to be at rest, to be alive as daughters, to transform our belief system, and ground our souls in truth. God wants us to know Him with our minds, our wills, and our emotions. He wants us to know Him experientially. But He does not want those things to lead us or be in charge of us. He wants our experiences, minds, wills, and emotions to be conducted by Him.

The Spirit of God makes the most healthy, alive, whole people because He teaches and trains us as the One who created us. He knows best what we need. He knows our strengths, weaknesses, and upbringings. We are only limited by our upbringing if we don't submit to His leadership. God will not invade or micromanage our lives. He will come when we say yes to Him, submit to Him, and honor Him above all other things. When we welcome Him to conduct our souls, we are no longer limited by how our dads did or didn't engage with us. We are free to be exactly who He created us to be.

ACTING
INTENTIONALLY

Sometimes I picture myself holding the question, pain, joy, relationship, or problem I'm dealing with in my hand and bringing it to the Father. Then looking into His face to see what expression He has about it.

It reminds me of the Bible's iconic phrase, "Seek His face."[6] As though a little girl were searching out her father's eyes to see his response to her scraped knee, her new piano song, her request to go to a friend's house, her "why?"

Bring any part of your soul—your thoughts, your own way, your feelings—before God and hold it there. Then allow Him to give your soul rest with His goodness.

ASK YOURSELF

- Which part of my soul tends to take leadership above the Holy Spirit? Mind (how I think and perceive things), will (my way of doing things), or emotion (what I'm feeling right now)? How do I let God train me in these areas?

- Am I allowing God and His Word to define what I love and value because I've experienced Him and His Word? Or am I letting my own experiences and what I love and value define how I follow God?

- How does the goodness of God change the way I look at my life today?

BUT AS
MANY AS
RECEIVED HIM,
TO THEM HE
GAVE THE RIGHT
TO BECOME

children of God.

JOHN 1:12 (NKJV)

processing

UNDERSTANDING OUR
CHILDHOOD BELIEFS AND
PRESENT REACTIONS

Have you ever wondered how to overcome lies? Especially those that drive you to habits, feelings, attitudes, or thoughts that feel hard to kick? I certainly have. Maybe you wonder how to recognize lies in the first place. Or why or how they got there.

I was recently talking with a man who has helped war veterans work through the trauma they experienced in battle.[1] As he talked with veterans about the horrific scenes of war, they obviously had to face painful memories. But he said their breakthrough often wouldn't come until they dug deeper.

This man went on to explain that we interpret nearly all our current circumstances through the lens of what we learned to believe in our hearts before the age of twelve and some within our teen years. When the veterans named the emotions that came from their painful memories, those emotions eventually led back to childhood memories where they felt the same way, even if the circumstances were entirely different. When they came to understand what they believed as a child, suddenly they had what it took to look at the war memories, see them, grieve them, forgive, and move toward healing.

As we've discussed, because our dads are often a large part of our developmental years, they can majorly affect our belief system. If they were absent during our childhood years, this can also affect what we believe about ourselves, God, or others. Our dads are not perfect, and the way we perceive them isn't either, so we may have some core lies from our relationships with them. How do we deal with these in healthy ways, without blaming them or overemphasizing the relationship?

As promised, I'll just tell you a little about my own process.

GETTING PAST WHAT WE KNOW
TO UNDERSTAND WHAT WE BELIEVE

You know that beautiful promise in Romans 8 that nothing can separate us from the love of God?[2] Because I believe the Word of God, I would have told you I believed that promise. And I did, with my intellect, which knew the truth, and my will, which I forced to act accordingly. But my mind and emotions were still being controlled by a fundamental lie, so my soul could not rest in this truth. God brought some circumstances into my life in order to unwrap what I believed on a heart level.

One morning several years ago, I was pondering father-daughter relationships as I brushed my teeth. That day I had an appointment with my counselor friend to ask her some questions about these father-daughter relationships . . . so that I could help others with their own questions, of course.

As I brushed, it dawned on me that there were some parts of God as a Father that I didn't truly know. I knew I believed those things about Him with my mind, but I realized it wasn't rooted in the kind of heart-based faith that comes from experience.

Sometimes girls with good dads have to experience a bit of a crisis in order to truly come to know God as a Father. My dad had represented God to me in beautiful ways. So much so that I sometimes felt my dad loved me more than God could. I reasoned, "My dad can't see inside me. God can." And I wasn't sure if someone could love what I often saw inside myself.

I finished brushing, then placed both hands on the edge of the vanity, looking myself in the face. I prayed, "God, help me know you as *Father.*"

I'm amazed by the power of an honest prayer. When we recognize that our experience with God is not lining up with what He says about Himself, it's powerful to be honest about that. Then ask Him to reveal whatever is keeping us from knowing Him in truth.

I left my house to meet with my friend. She saw right through me. She could see the places I didn't know the Father, even if I could tell you all about Him—in King James Version, if you'd like. She could see it in my stress. In the undertones of condemnation as I talked. In the fear that would subtly flash across my eyes. In the hard work I was pumping into believing, loving, and knowing my God, but not being able to taste and see what I was looking for. She could see it in the way I fearfully fought for connection with Him, instead of loving the One whose love I can never be separated from.

Somehow, she pulled it out of me. I was "asking for a friend," but she didn't buy it. I loved God. I knew His love. But as I let myself be honest, I realized I felt a wall between Him and me. Like there was something keeping me from truly knowing, in my heart, all that I knew in my head to be true about God as a Father. The stress in my busy season made me even more aware of this disconnection.

After I explained the wall and distance I felt from God, my friend asked me how that made me feel. I named emotions like loneliness, fear, and rejection. Then she asked, "What comes to mind when you focus on those feelings?"

As naturally as peanut butter pairs with jelly, a cluster of memories popped into my mind. It's called association. Kind of like when my mom buys the hairspray I used as a child. When I smell it, I'm suddenly in the bathroom of our old bus, watching in the mirror as my mom put my hair in a bun, and probably complaining that it didn't feel "right." Our mind associates smells, sights, tastes, and emotions with memories from the past.

The memories that popped in my head that day were from times I had failed my dad in some way. I didn't think they were a huge deal.

To me, they were justified responses. That was my adult interpretation of the memories. But my little girl heart didn't know that. It just knew rejection and distance.

It's important to note that perceived hurt can feel as real as intended hurt. Often parents don't intend to hurt us, but our hearts don't know the difference. As young girls, all we knew is what we experienced, so we need to be honest with what we perceived from those experiences so we can connect them to the truth.

Sitting with my friend, I remembered times when my dad was frustrated with me because I was late or forgot something important. Sometimes, when I failed my dad in some way, his response was to remain silent and remove himself from me for a while. We'd always apologize for bad attitudes and actions after some time. But as a little girl, I started to believe that if I failed, I was unlovable and worthy to be punished with distance—cue stress in my relationship with God.

When I failed God in some way, I knew that I could repent and my relationship with Him would be restored. But I felt subconscious pressure to perform for God, in fear that I would experience distance from Him if I didn't—even if I knew in my head that nothing could separate me from His love.

As I described a few of the scenes from my childhood relationship with my dad, my friend asked me to name the emotions those memories caused me to feel.

I used words like unloved, abandoned, and rejected.

"And why did his distance and silent treatments make you feel unloved, abandoned, and rejected?" she asked.

I concluded, "Because if I fail, I won't be loved."

There it was. The statement of belief. Even if I knew my dad loved me. Even if I knew God loved me. Even if I knew nothing could separate me from the love of God. As a young girl, in those small, defining moments, I took on a belief about myself that affected all my relationships. No matter what I knew intellectually, my heart was informing the rest of my soul to do whatever it took to avoid failure. It was exhausting.

In other words, my core belief was informing the rest of my soul how to avoid feeling something I didn't enjoy—punishment by distance and being unloved. The obvious conclusion was to perform in such a way that the other party wouldn't need to remove themselves from me. My soul rose to the challenge of pleasing and performing for God, my dad, and others, so I would feel worthy of love and close to them.

You may be wondering, *Isn't it a good thing to want to please God and press toward that goal?* Yes, absolutely. But Romans 14:23 says that everything that is not of faith (belief in truth) is sin. If my motivations for pleasing God were rooted in a lie, then, even if my intentions were good, the drive behind them was rooted in an agreement with the enemy instead of God.

> THERE IS A DIFFERENCE BETWEEN FEARING GOD AND BEING AFRAID OF BEING UNLOVED.

I believe strongly in the fear of God. There is a difference between fearing God and being afraid of being unloved. I believe a father-daughter relationship is one of the best pictures of what the fear of God looks like. As we discussed in the previous chapter, when loving discipline is paired with affection, approval, and acceptance, there is a beautiful paradox. We experience reverence and fear mixed with perfect safety, and freedom mixed with accountability.

There's a big difference between a girl who feels disapproval and therefore tries to win approval, and a daughter who feels approved of and responds in honor toward that love. It all has to do with motivation. When we're afraid of being unloved, 1 John 4 says we do not *know* God, who is love.[3] But when we fear God, we are free to fear nothing else.

Once I understood my underlying belief, I presented that lie to the Lord and asked Him, "Jesus, what do You want me to know about this?" Even though I intellectually knew nothing could separate me from the love of God, I didn't believe it at a heart level because of a lie that was embedded there. Simply being honest about this lie and presenting it to God changed me. The Spirit of God came into my mind, will, and emotions, quietly uprooted that lie, and transformed my soul to understand the truth about who the Father is.

After holding the memories and lies in the presence of God, I sensed a shift in my heart. The Spirit had done His work, bringing my belief into alignment with His Word through personal revelation. Transformation to the core. Tasting and seeing real love, not just convincing myself I'm loved.

As the root lie was replaced with His truth, my soul felt new life. I no longer needed my will to make me perform better. It was now motivated by loving God. My mind was renewed to think differently about why I do what I do. It no longer needed to associate the negative emotion to each similar circumstance that entered my life. My emotions could settle, even under pressure, because they weren't having to signal alerts to do whatever it took to keep from feeling unloved.

Forgiveness came next. It was important for me to forgive my dad for what was said and done, but also for how those things made me feel. "I forgive my dad for being frustrated, silent, and distant when I failed him, and for how that made me feel unloved, abandoned, and rejected."

Sometimes when we come to forgiveness, it feels hard to know if it's coming from our heart. Sometimes the protective tool of bitterness makes it hard to move past a situation. When we feel hesitation to let go of bitterness, it's usually because there's a lie attached to it. For instance, "If I let go of my bitterness, the same bad things will happen again." Or, "If I let go of my bitterness, that person won't be held accountable." Once God speaks truth into these lies, forgiveness flows from our hearts more freely.

That day my friend started me on a journey of personal growth, not one of blaming my dad or pointing out the ways he hurt me. Yes, because my dad was a huge part of my childhood years, he does come up in the memories where lies were formed. But he also comes up in the memories where truth was formed. Learning to process well is not about who did it or what happened, but about connecting to God for who He truly is.

I am learning to walk more honestly as I process before God and to ask myself why I do what I do. When I react in a conversation, or overcommit to people out of obligation, or feel stressed, or can't sleep, or shut down, or can't seem to forgive someone from my heart, I ask myself what is motivating me. What lie is keeping me from walking in all the freedom and fullness of being a daughter of God?

PAIN HURTS, LIES HAUNT

I want to note that there are seasons of tension, pressure, growth, and loss that have nothing to do with lies. They're just plain hard, exhausting, or difficult. There is both truth-based and lie-based pain, but we rarely experience anything that doesn't have a mixture of both.

I remember a time of personal loss when it was important for me to truly grieve, to hold questions in the presence of God, to lay awake at night in the disappointment and not just try to be positive and get over it. But there was also a time to recognize when my pain was not from the loss but from lies I was already believing, which the loss had triggered. Grieving the loss of something dear to me is different than believing lies like "God gives good to everyone but me," or "I have to fix this circumstance," or "This loss makes me worthless." Often the pain that lingers from loss, disappointment, and hurt has more to do with lies than the loss itself. But both are important to recognize and work through.

Bringing those lies into the presence of God didn't make my situation easy, but it made my process so different. When we mix truth with our loss and pain, somehow, someway, there is also joy. There is also a connection to God and others on deeper highs because we've experienced deeper lows. There is power in truth, not to make things better but to put our souls at rest. And God is gracious enough to allow us to walk in this as a process and lifestyle. He is gracious enough to bring the circumstances we need in order to unpack any belief that is not rooted in truth, so we can know Him and allow Him to live His life through us.

Our experiences do give opportunities for us to believe lies in our pain, disappointments, rejections, and misunderstandings. But our circumstances do not have to remain defined by the lies we believe. The pain that haunts us is often because of the lies we believe more than the circumstances themselves.

Our responsibility is to recognize the lies we agreed with and then agree with the truth instead. We don't need to defend or take responsibility for the other person's actions. We take responsibility for the lies we believed. When we're honest about it, and then hold it before God and His Word, we can know the power of overcoming. But if we never recognize it in the first place, we keep pressing on, blaming others, or trying to overcome with our own ideas and tools, missing the ways we could know the freedom of truth.

Norm Wakefield has a famous line that goes, "We live what we believe; all the rest is just religious talk."[4] Sometimes knowing what to do can blind us from what we're actually doing. Sometimes knowing what to think can blind us from understanding what we truly believe. Someone can tell us the truth until they're blue in the face, but if we're not living it and experiencing rest from it, we are not truly believing it.

Let's get honest with God. Let's give Him the opportunity to speak truth to us personally through His Word and Spirit. This truth we're talking about isn't just any convenient "personal truth" that allows us to do or feel what we want. It is truth that comes from someone who has the authority to define what is true.

FREED BY TRUTH

Many of us know we want to be people who agree with truth, not lies. However, it can be discouraging to continually be convincing ourselves of truth without experiencing the freedom of truth. I'm learning that when Jesus sets us free, we no longer need to be in constant cycles of defeat with the same lies. When He does the work of transforming us, it's the eternal, lasting kind of freedom, not the kind of "freedom" we can muster on a good day when we're feeling strong.

A faith in Christ that sets us free involves our personal choice, but not our personal strength. Faith in Christ is a choice to come into agreement with what He says is true so He can live His life through us in power. Our faith will be strong when He is the one informing us of the truth. The Greek word "faith" in the Bible boils down to being persuaded about something.[5] We will be persuaded by whoever we give the authority to define what is true.

No personal pep talks, counselors, mentors, pastors, or friends can ultimately convince us of the truth. These things can help, but it is through the personal revelation of Christ that we will be persuaded of the truth.

Coming up with our own truth will not set us free. A prisoner could sit in her locked cell, close her eyes, and tell herself she's been released from prison. But the reality is, the only way she will be released from prison is if a judge—an authority—says she is free to go. No matter what she tells herself, her reality doesn't change. Unless someone in authority says it first.

Because of the Cross, we have an authority that redefines what is true about our stories and identities. Jesus has said we can go free. He has the authority to say this, because he has taken our prison sentence on Himself. Which means, the only authority the enemy ever has is given to him when we agree with one of his lies. The level of rest in our souls will show who we are making the authority of our beliefs.

We don't come to the freedom of truth because our minds think it makes sense. Or because we will ourselves to freedom. Or because our emotions feel a certain level of happiness. No, we are set free because of the authority of the shed blood of Jesus. We experience this lasting freedom when the Holy Spirit personally reveals how the work of the Cross brings truth to our individual lies. When we agree with truth, the Holy Spirit can conduct our souls instead of our souls trying to showcase the fruit of the Holy Spirit by our own strength.

You may ask, "How do I hear from the Holy Spirit?" As I talk with other believers, I'm finding that we often hear from God in different ways, and sometimes we hear from Him differently in different seasons of life. This idea can hardly be put in a box. But when He speaks, we are changed. No matter how we hear Him, it's important that we believe He *wants* to talk to us. Sometimes our own lies and living keep us from hearing Him. He is constantly working and speaking. It is our intentional awareness of this that moves us to hear and be changed.

When the Spirit speaks to me, I don't often hear clear words. Usually it's a simple sense, nudge, or shift in my spirit like a "still, small voice."[6]

Feeling the nudge of the Spirit can be as simple as a split-second thought. Like a soft breeze you feel but don't hear. The more we practice listening and seeking Him in our everyday decisions, the more we know how to respond with a quicker "yes" to agree with truth. The Holy Spirit always aligns with God's Word and character, so we can be secure in listening to His voice when Scripture backs up what we sense. It's so vital that we immerse ourselves in the Word. We will never be truly freed by creating our own experience. We don't need to hear from Him in a certain way, we simply need to be aware of His presence, read His Word, and be attentive to how He is working in us and around us.

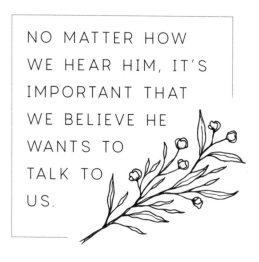

NO MATTER HOW WE HEAR HIM, IT'S IMPORTANT THAT WE BELIEVE HE WANTS TO TALK TO US.

We can sense His voice as we ponder in bed before falling asleep at night. We can hear Him singing over us[7] as we wake up with a song of worship running through our heads. We can hear Him speak through sermons or words from a friend. We hear Him when we pray, then listen.

Have you ever known a moment of healing as you were on your knees before God in prayer? That's the Holy Spirit. Have you had a thought strike you as you were on your morning jog? Heard a "still, small voice" in the aisle of the grocery store and became aware of God with you? Had a verse leap off the page of your Bible? If so, then you know what it's like to hear the voice of God.

Romans 8:14 says, "For all who are led by the Spirit of God are sons [and daughters] of God." It is the Holy Spirit who leads us into the freedom and power of being daughters of God. He will gladly reveal Himself to us as we engage in the daily process of transformation.

This process will include choosing who has the authority to define what is true in our hearts, when our feelings and thoughts contradict what God says. We simply need to be honest with God about this. Ask Him questions, seek His heart and Word, and give Him the authority to transform us with truth.

When we look to Him for truth, transformation, and overcoming power, we no longer have to work for our own freedom. The work has already been done on the Cross. We simply agree with the Word of God, and allow the Spirit to give us personal revelation for how the Cross changes our lives, lies, and relationships today.

ACTING
INTENTIONALLY

The next time you feel unsettled emotions inside you, pause and name them. So often we subconsciously stuff them down and keep moving on. Once you've named them, dig deeper. What's really going on? What lie is in the undercurrent of what you're dealing with? Could it be tied to a core childhood belief?

See if a memory connects with the emotions you named. Ask yourself, "Why do/did I feel this way?" Name the lie. Even if it sounds cliche or too extreme for the situation. Name what you believed before you knew better.

Then ask Him these questions:

- Jesus, what truth do you want me to know about this lie?
- God, what do you want me to know about You right now?

Allow Him to shift and move whatever He needs to, in His way. His presence and Word will be where you experience the freedom of truth in every part of your being. Choose to agree with Him.

ASK YOURSELF

o How might the beliefs I formed in my childhood affect how I'm viewing my present situations?

o Is there a disconnect between what the Bible says about Father God and how I truly experience Him?

o What honest prayer do I need to pray today?

o In what ways does the Holy Spirit speak to me personally?

o Am I blaming my dad for how I'm living, or am I taking responsibility for the lies I believe? Am I choosing to agree with Christ and truth?

WHERE ARE THE PEOPLE READY

TO DO HARD AND

holy things?

ANN VOSKAMP[1]

CHAPTER 5

submission

THE BRAVE HEART OF A DAUGHTER

Seven days of extravagant wonder. Pillars and floors hewn from pure marble. Drapes of white, blue, and purple cascaded from silver rods, blowing as wind whisked through the court in the king's garden. Everyone in Susa was invited to this unprecedented event. The fine wine normally rationed was served bottomless in gold goblets.

This seven-day party was the climax of a 180-day feast for the royals, which was held to show off the splendor of dear King Ahasuerus's kingdom. The scenes described in Esther chapter one make me want to get on that king's event team. My mind is forever taken by picturing what this party would have been like. It sounds like they nailed the decor, the food, and the mood. But I honestly think the event team could've used me. I would've made sure good entertainment was lined up and maybe saved Queen Vashti some trouble.

To close off these lavish days of feasting and celebration, the men with bottomless gold goblets summoned Vashti to come before them and show off her renowned beauty. Can you imagine your beauty being the closing show? There's debate about what the king implied by "showing her beauty," but, whatever the request meant, Vashti's refusal seems to signify that she considered it degrading.

I don't know what Vashti's motivations were, but the king's men seemed to take her refusal as having all the makings of a movement. They reasoned, "The queen's behavior will be made known to all women, causing them to look at their husbands with contempt, since they will say, 'King Ahasuerus commanded Queen Vashti to be brought before him, and she did not come'" (Esther 1:17).

Their solution was to ban the queen from ever coming before the king again and to choose another who was "better than she" to take her spot. They hoped the result would go like this: "So when the decree made by the king is proclaimed . . . all women will give honor to their husbands, high and low alike."[2]

This pagan culture cared a lot about authority and honor. But I don't think they cared about it for the same reasons God cares about it. From this story, it seems women were viewed as objects for men's pleasure and forced to give honor to the men in their lives even if the men didn't return love or honor back to them. The king and all his men took the idea of authority and warped it into a process that fit their own agenda.

I don't know what I would've done if I were Vashti. I'm not sure who all was right or wrong in this story. But I know that the women in the story of Esther were greatly affected by the authorities in their culture and era, just like each of us is today.

AUTHORITY BUILDS
THE HEART OF A DAUGHTER

One could hardly talk about dads and avoid the obvious: they're the boss of you. Or at least, they once were. How do you respond when you hear the word *authority?* Some of you may assume a fetal position, while others may just think it's a fancy Bible word for the people in charge.

Each heart brings its own experience to the table. Depending on the character of the pastor, police officer, or parent in our lives, we each inwardly create our own definition of authority.

Often God's very good ideas get warped by the agenda of the enemy or the untransformed hearts of men. What is meant to be a blessing becomes a curse when the process is motivated by selfishness, sin, religion, or just plain ignorance.

It's like when I first started baking. I'm a bit of an Amelia Bedelia in the kitchen—a little of this, a little of that, and hope for the best. Actually, not just hope, pray. I've had so many kitchen fails that I started praying over the goods. The bread would knead in the mixer, and I'd lay hands on it, believing for a miracle.

It eventually occurred to me that I was asking amiss, because I was skipping the process and praying He'd cover for it. I used to hate recipe instructions. How hard could it be? Put it all in an electric mixer and crank that puppy to the max. What could go wrong? A few flopped recipes and a nice mom who paid a visit to the kitchen helped me answer that question.

We tend to do this with God's good recipes. The ones with splatters and faded writing, used by many to enjoy flavor and nourishment. We put the ingredients in, but don't do it the way He would. We don't get the yeast-to-water-temperature relationship, the egg-to-beating connection, or the point behind sifting the flour. We buy the cheapest ingredients, throw them together, and miss quality and intention.

I think we also do this with authority. Eric Ludy wisely said, "The man-made stuff destroys when it overpowers the God-essentials."[3] God was the one who created authority structures and the ideas of obedience, submission, and honor. But man has often recreated these ideas into warped formulas and control, sometimes leaving us with a bad taste in our mouths.

Most of my experiences with authority have been positive. I have been surrounded by healthy, warm servant leaders who had my best interests in mind. I have valid reasons to believe the best about my authorities. Even so, I've had my days of resenting those authorities. I've also had days of idolizing authorities, taking their word almost above God's.

I had read all the Scriptures about honor and submission. I thought I understood my role as a daughter, and I did it. But eventually I wondered what I was supposed to think about *myself* in this mix. Underneath my "submission," I felt a little violated. Something inside me became afraid of submitting to others because it seemed like I would ultimately be unseen, unknown, or uncomfortable.

Sometimes we forget there is a difference between submission and shutting down. I haven't always remembered the difference. So I've wondered, can people honor their authorities and be healthy individuals? Or will they always be quietly hurting, inwardly half shut down? Can they live out what God called them to or only support what others are called to? What truly pleases God?

Maybe you haven't had these questions. Once I didn't either. I thought submitting to authority was clear and simple. But real life made me realize it doesn't always seem that way.

Now God's Word has informed my real life of this conclusion: the heart behind submission is far better than I ever imagined it would be. I've found it freeing and life-giving. I've found authority, honor, and submission have released me into God's big mission, giving me a small, vital role in it.

> SOMETIMES WE FORGET THERE IS A DIFFERENCE BETWEEN SUBMISSION AND SHUTTING DOWN.

Submission may be a word that's been used wrongly in your life. Perhaps it's been preached to create performance, devalue you, or beat you into place. I don't believe it was God's heart for you to experience authority this way.

My friend who mentors girls always says the word slow and broken: *sub*-mission. She wants them to remember, every time, what it really means and that it's a good thing. A Jesus thing. Broken up the way my friend says it, there's an emphasis on the prefix. *Sub,* as in under. Sub-merge, sub-marine, sub-way, sub-ject. All words that describe coming under something, someone, or some idea. This prefix is followed by the word mission. Sub-mission. Submission is putting ourselves under another's mission. Doesn't this definition sound a little different than how we sometimes perceive the word? I'm not entirely sure how all of this works, but I'm finding that submission to authority is not stuffy or stifling. It is the very thing that births the vivacious life of being part of a mission that's bigger than ourselves.

Everyone has a mission, whether they realize it or not. Our mission shows up in how we're using our time, interacting with the people around us, and spending our money. It shows up in the ideas we dream about and the subjects we talk about. A mission is, essentially, where someone is going and how they are planning to get there. There are selfish and selfless missions. A selfish mission centers around our fleshly desires to be comfortable, happy, and validated in the ways we think it best. A selfless mission is motivated by a purpose bigger than ourselves.

Coming under someone's mission means looking for ways we can support their values, help them get where they want to go, listen to their advice, and use our voice to help them see what they may not be able to see without us. God often refines our own mission by teaching us to engage with the mission of others.

To see this kind of sub-mission in action, let's pick up where we left off in the book of Esther. We now understand the political temperature of authority in Susa at large, where the story takes place. The leaders were taking good ideas about authority and honor and warping them to fit their own agenda. But then the narrative walks us right into the home of our girl, Esther, where authority looks just a little different.

Esther was, by definition, an orphan. Orphans are particularly close to the heart of God. He cares for the helpless who don't have the protection, nurture, and provision of a parent.[4] No child chooses this position. But in a spiritual sense, we are orphans until we make a choice.

Sadly, orphans often have to learn to fend for themselves, unless someone steps in with a rescue. They have to nurture themselves and fight for their own lives because no one else is doing it for them. Fundamentally, they have to serve their own mission, because they have to be in charge of their own survival.

When Adam and Eve took the first bite of the forbidden fruit, they chose their own mission instead of God's. They decided they would do what it took to provide for themselves and what they thought was good, instead of staying within God's mission for them. No orphan has ever chosen their lot in life. But in the spiritual sense,

Adam and Eve *chose* the life of orphans. We are all descendants of Adam and Eve, and so we all bear this sin nature. We are born fighting and fending for ourselves. Advocates of our own mission. Spiritual orphans.

When we have loving parents, they teach us, instead, that someone is fighting for us, calling us to life, nurturing and loving us, because we're their children. This is a physical picture of what happens in the spiritual realm when we choose Jesus. The Bible uses the analogy of adoption to help us understand what the Cross means in our lives.[5] We no longer have to fend and fight for ourselves. We no longer have to prove or protect ourselves. We no longer have to nurture and name ourselves according to what we think is good. We have Someone who's doing all that for us. Someone has stepped in to make us daughters.

Esther has the same story. Esther 2:7 says that her near relative, Mordecai, took her in "as his own daughter." Mordecai adopted Esther. He parented her, trained her, provided for her, and loved her as his own. Esther 2:20 says that "Esther obeyed Mordecai just as when she was brought up by him." These verses imply that Esther was trained, disciplined, and taught by Mordecai. Their relationship implies that he provided a place of safe belonging and love. They communicated out of a relationship of mutual trust and understanding. When discipline and training is paired with love and acceptance, the idea of submitting to that training is freeing.

When a daughter has been given value by a loving, strong father figure there is often a remarkable confidence and freedom to be herself within her submission. Healthy authority will nurture the girl for who she was made to be, helping her know she has something valuable to affect the world with. Esther was parented and loved well. But she also had to make the choice, in both her childhood and adulthood, to submit herself to authority. The choices came in moments when it must have looked and felt like authorities were making her life difficult.

Picture what the story of Esther would have looked like if a loving authority had not stepped into her life. Now picture your own life without your authorities. I am challenged to remember the simple gift of having someone parent me. Many of us take for granted the benefits of having two parents who intentionally trained us. In our fallen world, this is a gift I want to treasure with gratitude.

It's easy to believe the lie that we'd be freer, more ourselves, and more capable to fulfill our destinies if we could do without authorities in our lives. But Esther is a beautiful picture of the counter-truth to this lie. In order to be without authority, we take on the heart of a spiritual orphan. Authority and submission defused Esther's position as an orphan, and built in her the heart of a daughter. Because God offers adoption into His household, no matter our experiences, we always have the option to exchange our orphan heart for the heart of a daughter who is protected, valued, and plugged into a mission bigger than herself.

> IN A CULTURE THAT DIDN'T HONOR THE VOICES OF WOMEN, HER DEMEANOR OF SUBMISSION GAVE HER A VOICE.

Pretty, orphaned Esther placed herself under the mission of Mordecai. This heart posture followed her into the startling circumstances that would put her in a new world, away from the safety of her own subculture and connection to people who loved her. As you read the story of Esther, watch for her presence of mind, competence, wisdom, and courage. She seems to show all the signs of someone who is loved and confident in her position. Not someone who has to push her way through, fend for herself, or protect herself. In a culture that didn't honor the voices of women, her demeanor of submission gave her a voice.

THE MISSION OF GOD

Esther was taken from her safe, warm home, and neither she nor Mordecai could do anything about it. She was brought into the king's palace, along with all the other most beautiful virgins in the land, for a contest to see who would replace the gorgeous Vashti.

In this terrifying new circumstance, her response is fascinating. She sought out the mission of a new authority that she hadn't chosen and probably didn't want. Hegai was the eunuch in charge of all the potential future queens in their seven-month beauty regime. Esther 2:15 says, "When the turn came for Esther . . . to go in to the king, she asked for nothing except what Hegai the king's eunuch, who was in charge of the women, advised."

Esther had the freedom to choose whatever she wanted to prove herself to the king. But she seemed to be comfortable in her own skin, not needing to prove herself at all. She sought out the mission of her authority in this new place, even though I'm sure she wasn't a huge fan of her situation. You know what word the Bible uses to describe Esther's life in the middle of all these odd circumstances? Favor.

We probably all know what happened next: Esther was chosen to become queen. Then she took the counsel of her cousin-father and kept her nationality a secret from her new world. Next, a series of unfortunate events made that counsel a key player in the choices Esther would need to make. An obsessive, controlling leader set out to annihilate a people group who didn't want to follow the mission that started and ended with him. This targeted ethnic group just happened to be the Jews—Esther's people. The authoritarian leader, Haman, used some stealthy wording on the king and got him to sign a decree that would grant Haman permission to wipe this people group out. (Of course, the king had no idea this included his new queen.)

Mordecai's political involvement in Susa meant that he found out about this mess before Queen Esther did. He sent messengers to communicate with her about what was going on. Now, picture this scenario with me. It would seem like Mordecai's counsel about keeping her nationality a secret wasn't turning out the best. If I were Esther, I would be thinking, *If I would've told the king about my nationality in the first place, he probably wouldn't have signed that decree!*

Furthermore, the very reason the Jews were being targeted was because of Mordecai himself. He refused to bow to Haman, and because Haman obsessively needed to prove himself a leader, this triggered rash action. Again, if I were Esther, I probably would have been thinking, *You're the one who got us into this mess. Would it really be so terrible to bow to the guy? Surely, that would be a better answer than me risking my life!*

I don't know if Esther had any thoughts like this. If she did, she didn't show it or act on them. The first thing she did was listen to counsel. As if he were a sergeant in the secret lair of his camp, Mordecai laid out a battle plan for her. He gave her a choice. She wouldn't be disobedient if she chose another strategy. Mordecai knew the truth about risk and about choice. God is sovereign. He writes stories and redeems self-absorbed leadership decisions, but He invites us to use our voices to accomplish His mission. Instead of receiving this invitation, we often choose the battle plan that we think will save our necks.

Knowing this, Mordecai said something to Esther that is true about each of our stories. First, he reminded her that to try and save her life in this instance would just set her up for another chance at death. We miss that all the time. We try to preserve our lives and selves by rejecting anything that doesn't align with our mission to be comfortable, applauded, happy, or successful. We miss the fact that, if we don't enter into a mission bigger than ourselves at this turn, another "death" to those things is entirely possible. Submitting our own lives to receive the thoughts, counsel, and vision of our leaders can open our eyes to the bigger mission of God.

Then Mordecai told pretty Esther, "If you don't, someone else will." God's sovereign plan will come to pass whether we're interested in it or not. But He personally invites us into this plan. When we've been subject to the mission of our earthly authorities, we make ourselves ready for defining moments of being subject to God's mission, and sometimes we save a nation.

When Esther was presented with this opportunity, she was a woman about it. After she heard out her cousin-father, she checked in with the heart of God to see what His mission was. She didn't let the voice of her authority keep her from seeking God for herself, but she did take care to listen to it. Through messengers, she told Mordecai to have all the Jews pray and fast on behalf of this decision, and she and her maidens would do the same.

Queen Esther was in a hard place. This was sticky, risky, and a nightmare at best. She couldn't just casually chat with her husband about her heritage over coffee and toast in the morning. She had to be summoned by him. And it had been months since she was.

The rules of this kingdom were pretty straightforward—if you came to the king when he hadn't summoned you, you would be killed (even if you were cute). So basically, in order to honor the counsel of her father figure, she would have to disobey the rules of this kingdom and her husband. I think it would've been smart to pray that God would have the king summon her. Surely, that would be the safest solution. But that's not what she asked the people to fast for. She requested fasting and then said, "If I perish, I perish."[6]

Esther understood something here. Living for a mission bigger than ourselves is not always safe. But when we know who we are as daughters, and whose mission we're entering into, we can take risks in hard, unsafe places because we're taking risks from a love that casts out fear, instead of taking risks to prove ourselves. And usually the people around us will sense the difference.

This world doesn't always make decisions surrounding authority easy. Esther was about to break a rule and make an appeal to her authority, not so she could get something she wanted but because she chose a mission bigger than herself. She was using her voice not just for her good, but for the good of people who wouldn't have had a voice without her. If we ever feel God is asking us to break out of a mold, a cultural way of doing things, or a rule or idea that may not be godly or good, let's make sure we're doing so because of the gospel, not just to do what feels good to us.

When we think the mission of God does not align with the mission of our authorities, our greatest battle will be maintaining the heart of a daughter and not defaulting to self-protecting, putting ourselves back in the position of a spiritual orphan. A spiritual orphan is motivated by the fear of being unloved, along with a mistrust in God or others. A daughter is motivated by love and trust, which gives her a heart of confidence instead of self-dependence.

I have stood amazed next to women who have submitted hearts even in challenging circumstances with their authorities. The Holy Spirit has given powerful, profound wisdom for their unique situations, and I have witnessed the power of the gospel continually and radically transform their lives. I've watched them be bold in their pursuit of Christ, even if their authorities didn't understand. Some of them knew that doing what their authorities wanted would mean compromising the true gospel, so they had to choose God's mission above the mission of their authority. But all the while, I've seen them make intentional choices to honor the mission of these same authorities in whatever ways they could.

One common theme I saw in the lives of these women was this: favor. Even if they didn't have the relationship results they wanted, their heart posture of submitting to a larger mission allowed them to walk in a lifestyle of peace and power.

We should submit to our authorities because we are submitted to the larger mission of God, not just so we can feel good about ourselves. If we're more concerned about pleasing our dads than pleasing God, we're missing the heart of submission. There is a beautiful theme in the New Testament nearly every time the idea of submission to authority is mentioned.

"As to the Lord."

"In the Lord."

"As to the Lord and not to man."[7]

These ideas are linked to children and parents, husbands and wives, servants and masters, believer to believer. This is our grace. We submit to our dads *as to the Lord.*

Jesus did everything He did because of and for the Father. He centered His identity around being a son. Philippians 2:5–8 brings all of this full circle:

> "Have this mind among yourselves, which is yours in Christ Jesus, who, though he was in the form of God, did not count equality with God a thing to be grasped but emptied himself, by taking the form of a servant, being born in the likeness of men. And being found in human form, he humbled himself by becoming obedient to the point of death, even death on a cross."

Jesus knew who He was—God. He was equal with God. He didn't have to "grasp" for this position. It was who He was, and He knew it. From this settled knowledge, He willingly chose to be a servant. To be humble. To be obedient. To come under God's greater mission.

When we know our position as daughters in Christ, we have the freedom to serve, honor, and prefer others like He did because we have no need to prove, promote, or protect ourselves. We have a Father who is doing that for us. When we know we are daughters, we can freely come underneath others without our love, identity, or position being shaken. When

> WE CAN USE SUBMISSION IN OUR HOMES AS A LAUNCHING PAD FOR A MISSION-FILLED LIFE.

we know who we are as daughters, we can act with the boldness of Esther to do hard, risky things for the mission of God. We can use submission in our homes as a launching pad for a mission-filled life.

Esther's story is a little crazy. We romanticize it, because we've seen the VeggieTales version and have probably heard the iconic story from children's books since we were little. But she did not have easy circumstances. She had to make complicated decisions. You may be able to relate.

Esther listened to advice, but she also broke some cultural rules. She risked everything for something bigger than herself without any promise of things turning out well. She didn't expect to have her story told thousands of years after it took place. She made her choice and said, "If I perish, I perish."

Then she showed us that the heart of submission may teach us how to use our voice, even when it feels like no one is listening. She showed us the power of what can happen when our hearts are anchored into an authority bigger than us.

Esther reminds us that submission does not mean staying cozy at home, doing whatever we're told to do without questioning, but rather it's giving up our own way so that we are ready to use our voice, wisdom, and courage with purpose. We are not promised that our authorities will respond well to our heart of submission, but we always have the opportunity to be submitted to God's mission. The hearts of daughters are the hearts that risk without fear, because they know the love of a father who calls them to live for a mission bigger than themselves.

ACTING
INTENTIONALLY

A few years back, I had a personal revival when it came to how I view authorities. I thought I totally got what it meant to submit and honor. But often, even if I did something they suggested, I inwardly thought I had a better way of doing things. I had an underlying chip on my shoulder, feeling like doing things the way my authorities suggested made me a martyr to their ways.

So I decided to test the waters. Instead of always giving a counter opinion, I started being willing to do things in a different way than I normally would. I started being willing to do things simply because it supported the mission of the person I was serving. It was remarkably freeing. It taught me that there is more than one good way to do things, and mine isn't automatically the best. Next time you think to yourself, *I have a better way of doing this,* try fully giving yourself to the way they would do it and just see if you won't be a little more free.

There is a flip side to this challenge. Sometimes helping someone in their mission means using your voice like Esther did. Maybe you tend to keep your thoughts and opinions to yourself. Instead, next time your authority has an idea, consider that you may have something valuable to say to further their mission or help them see a new perspective.

ASK YOURSELF

○ How would I approach my life differently if I believed I didn't have to fight for a position, and lived from a position in Christ instead?

○ Am I continually fighting for my own way of doing things, or am I willing to submit to the mission of others in authority over me?

○ When was the last time I took a risk, allowing myself to try something and possibly fail, because I was walking with the confidence of a loved daughter?

He is no fool

WHO GIVES WHAT HE CANNOT KEEP

TO GAIN WHAT HE CANNOT LOSE.

JIM ELLIOT[1]

CHAPTER 6

honor

HOW ATTITUDE AFFECTS OUR DREAMS

My grandma is from the generation that values china cabinets full of dishes to pass down as heirlooms. And she's serious about the passing down part. She has a set for each child—boys and girls.

I remember the day we stood in Grandma's kitchen, slowly lowering delicate dishes from her china cabinet. We found the ones with my dad's name markered on masking tape underneath them. There were dinner, salad, soup, and dessert plates, cups, saucers, meat platters, and serving bowls.

We asked Grandma what kind of occasions these dishes had been used for. It would've been nice to hear about birthday dinners spread on the table, bridal showers for her daughters, or tea parties with her grandma friends. But, no, they had never been eaten off of, never used to serve anyone. Their life story was store-to-cabinet. In their place at the table, there was the fleeting life of the paper product, the everlasting stamina of the Tupperware bowl, and the timeless presence of the Corelle plate.

My mom is both from a different generation and plagued with a different disposition than my quaint, orderly grandma. She is the queen of making every day full of things that aren't "everyday." When I was a little girl, she made the decision to use her wedding dishes regularly, instead of storing them away safely. She reasoned, "No one will appreciate them like we will, so we may as well be the ones to use them." We would set the table with a dressy cloth and her wedding dishes for Sundays, company, special dinners before Dad would go on trips, Valentine's Day, brunch with ladies, and birthday parties with my little posse of friends.

The gold-rimmed goblets and glasses broke from her young children clearing the table and loading them into the dishwasher. After twenty-five years of marriage, five children, and six moves, all the goblets are broken, and only one gold-rimmed glass stands tall and companionless in our cupboard. Most of the plates are still intact, though one had to be super-glued after a clean break down the center. Mom always sets that one at her seat when we have company over. There are some teacups missing, but most of the other pieces are accounted for. The elegant silverware with gold fan-like tips was kept separate from the everyday silverware for years. But eventually a household silverware famine (who in the world knows how these things disappear?) made Mom dump the fancy stuff in with all the rest.

SHE PLACES VALUE ON US BY USING WHAT IS VALUABLE TO HER TO SERVE US.

I probably won't get a full set of china from my mom. But if even one plate remains unbroken, the impact and memories wrapped up in that single dish would cause a knot in my throat.

My mom was intentional about meals. They weren't just for eating, they were for connecting. She wasn't trying to save everything for a special time—she was making any ordinary time special. Often, when we ate off of her nice dishes, we were being served leftovers. It was her secret strategy to make it feel like more than it was. My mom's goal for getting out the good dishes was to honor her family. She places value on us by using what is valuable to her to serve us.

Not everyone will fuss like Mom did, or appreciate it. But packing my grandmother's unused china into boxes taught me a life lesson.

My grandma's value for dishes was all about passing something on. And so the mission became about keeping them safe. Treasuring them for the purpose of saving their life. My mom valued dishes too. But her mission for them was to be enjoyed, to be an avenue for cultivating relationships and memories. And because that was the mission of the dishes, the fact that most of them are chipped or broken doesn't matter. Saving them would have defeated their purpose.

Neither of these values was wrong. But both values determined the use of their dishes. I often value my own life like my grandma valued her dishes. I value the saving of my life instead of giving it away. My dishes can be my talents, gifts, and abilities, along with my dreams about how to live them out. My dishes can include my time and resources.

I value the potential of what my dishes could be used for. But this value sometimes makes me tuck them away safely, saving them for the ideal situations that excite and validate me. An attitude of honor for others moves me to take my best dishes out of the cupboard and use what God has given me. I show them their value by bringing my best to the everyday situations instead of only saving my best for special occasions.

The very thing we think we're doing to save our precious lives, dreams, goals, and gifts can sometimes be the thing keeping us from living them. "Whoever would save his life will lose it, but whoever loses his life for my sake will find it" (Matthew 16:25). Jesus said these famous words more than two thousand years ago, and I still need to hear them daily. Without realizing it, we may be losing the opportunity to use our gifts and talents in the one life we have. *Why aren't things happening?* we ask. *Why aren't my dreams coming true, God? Why aren't people seeing these valuable dishes that are mine?*

You know how Ephesians 6:3 promises that when we honor our parents things will be well with us? Meaning there will be favor and blessing over our endeavors, tasks, and life. I think this is largely because honor calls us to live today with the best of what we've got. When we honor others, we are saying, "I will bring the best of me to the table to serve you." This attitude is what gets us places. We should no longer wait for favor to spring upon us in some special occasion. We ought to live in a way that our lives are marked by favor in every-day interactions and tasks, because we've chosen to honor others by giving our best in whatever relationship or situation we're in.

Sometimes honoring others will wage war on our own, precious ways. But we often miss the gift in this. When we fight against anything that stands in the way of our own mission, we often develop the very attitudes that keep us from being credible for the dreams we desire.

There have been times when I named dreams and goals I had, and my dad or other authorities cautioned them. There have been times when I felt my gifts or talents were unseen and passed over by the people in charge.

But, later on, I often see that these cautions and oversights were more about the character that still needed to be developed in me than about the abilities or dreams involved. This taught me to focus more on how I'm living than what I'm doing.

If we are waiting for our gifts to be appreciated or our dreams to come true, it may be time to start looking for ways we're not practicing the attitude of honor, especially with our authorities. There is a saying that goes like this, "People may not remember exactly what you did or what you said, but they will always remember how you made them feel."[2] People often feel our attitudes before they notice our abilities. Honor reminds us to focus more on *how* we do something than on *what* we do. How we serve leftover casserole may just be the thing that matters to God the most.

I think this is what Ephesians 6 implies. Things "going well" with us doesn't mean we won't ever have any chipped dishes, but it means there will be favor over our lives, allowing us to live purposefully and fully because the dishes are out of the cupboard to serve others. Honor moves us from a focus on how our lives will turn out to a focus on how we're treating others in the process. We value the people around us by serving them with the valuables that God has entrusted to our care.

Honoring others doesn't mean we should disregard our abilities and dreams so that everyone else can live theirs. Quite the opposite. It invites us to start using our abilities and living our dreams today with an attitude to serve the people around us. We can get our best dishes out now with whoever is around us, including our dads.

THE ATTITUDE OF HONOR

Honor implies more than obedience. It implies attitude. The way our hearts are bent toward others. It suggests that we place a high value on someone or something. A high value on their opinions. Their way of thinking. Their potential. Their goals. Their hearts. The image they were made in. Do our dads feel this from us?

I hope you understand, honoring someone who is acting dishonorably does not mean we're saying their actions are honorable. Honor is not saying, "You get to do whatever you want in this relationship, because I am committed to honoring you." There may be times we need to set up boundaries in relationships with an authority if there is not returned honor and love. But often, honor means doing what we can to communicate that we value the person and their position.

> HONOR MEANS DOING WHAT WE CAN TO COMMUNICATE THAT WE VALUE THE PERSON AND THEIR POSITION.

Hebrews 13:17 says, "Obey your leaders and submit to them, for they are keeping watch over your souls, as those who will have to give an account. Let them do this with joy and not with groaning, for that would be of no advantage to you."

Are you making your dad's leadership role a joy? How do you handle the tasks, interactions, and involvement in your dad's life, world, or home? How do you handle your dad's mission? Have you ever thought to consider what it is? What are his goals for his family, his business, his lifestyle, his church, and his daughter?

You may or may not be able to agree with his mission. You may or may not feel called in the same direction as his goals. But that is not the question here. As my dad always says, honor has nothing to do with agreeing. Are you living in an attitude of honor within your interactions with him? In the places you can agree with your dad's mission, run with it. Advance the places your life touches his goals. This may be in business, in attitude, in church, or in your home. When we bring our best to our dad's big responsibility of being our authority, Hebrews 13 reminds us that this benefits us as well as our dad.

THE CHOICE TO HONOR

Remember the story of twelve-year-old Jesus teaching in the temple? I was around that age when I felt stirrings for what I was called to, what I wanted to do, and who I wanted to be. I was awakened to the desire to make my own decisions and start doing the things I once only pretended. I think this is a natural shift we feel as we begin to head toward adulthood.

Imagine being twelve-year-old you in a setting like Jesus in the temple.[3] He's asking good questions and speaking about things that have probably been in His heart for years already. And the adults around Him are impressed, listening to Him and engaging with Him. If this were me, I would be atop my high horse, glad everyone was finally seeing the wonder of me.

Picture this scene. Jesus is away from his parents, in a place where His thoughts are being heard and noticed. His gifts are being seen and respected. Then, suddenly, Mom and Dad show up, and they're more than a little miffed. They question His actions and scold Him in front of the bigwig leaders who were in deep discussion with Him. Wouldn't you think they were being overprotective? Wouldn't you be annoyed that they treated you like you were twelve when others were treating you like an adult?

Jesus answered them by saying, "Why were you looking for me? Did you not know that I must be in my Father's house?"

Then it goes from bad to worse. The Bible says they didn't understand Him. I hate being misunderstood, especially by my parents.

But do you know what Jesus did? He would've had the right to be superior to His imperfect parents (what with Him being God and all). Instead, Luke 2:51 says, "And he went down with them and came to Nazareth and was submissive to them." Then, in verse 52, the Bible uses the same word for Jesus as it used for Esther: favor. "And Jesus increased in wisdom and in stature and in favor with God and man."

All throughout our lives we will have moments when we feel ready. When we go to the temple and we know we're hitting some kind of stride. When we feel fully adult, fully called, and fully capable. When we want to be in charge of ourselves. There is certainly a healthy independence each of us should experience as we grow older. But, often, the key to favor in our lives is choosing to learn when we feel we know it all. Choosing to honor when we feel like we'd be the better boss. Because what we sow is what we will reap. If we're honoring others by serving them with our gifts now, there's a good chance others will begin to honor us too.

Sometimes when we feel most ready, God invites us to learn from others so He can decide when we're ready. Jesus experienced this. The perfect twelve-year-old God was submissive to His imperfect earthly mother and father.

Jesus got it: we don't become adults by acting like children. We become adults by living with a childlike heart and adultlike responsibility. The Bible talks about the importance of remaining in childlikeness.[4] But it also talks about growing up into maturity in Christ.[5] Honor invites us into the creative tension of a childlike heart that stays open, trusting, curious, loving, and learning, paired with a mature heart that owns choices and walks in the freedom that comes with responsibility.

A child eats brussels sprouts in a highchair, crying and prolonging the process, with an irrational terror of death-by-vegetable. A good parent will discipline the child to understand obedience even when it isn't comfortable. But that obedience is entirely up to the way the parent chooses to set the standard. A child doesn't have a choice but to submit.

But an adult does have a choice. We often begin to feel this choice when we're around the age Jesus was in the temple. We begin to feel the natural instinct to be responsible for ourselves. To do the things we were created for. Jesus could have acted like a child and begrudgingly gone back with his parents, muttering the whole time that they just didn't understand Him. They just didn't understand God's will for His life. Instead, He acted like an adult and chose to honor them.

Honor moves us beyond childlike obedience. When we were children, we didn't have a choice in who our parents were or how they parented us. We had no choice but to be obedient to that parenting. But, as young adults, we're given a choice in how we respond to them. We are no longer a victim in a highchair. We have a choice in how we interact with them. We have the privilege of choosing to invite our dads into our lives, decisions, and dreams.

HONORING OUR DAD'S VOICE

When we choose adultlike attitudes, we help invite our dads to be counselors who work with our hearts. A father's counsel is not meant to control our lives or take the place of the voice of God, but it is a beautiful tool God uses to help us make decisions and learn life lessons. We won't always agree with our dads when we have conversations about where we want to go or what we want to do, but we can still value their voice.

I remember once when I was in the middle of making a difficult life decision. I had been dreaming and praying about a cool opportunity that would allow me to use my gifts and talents in ways I loved. My parents weren't sure how they felt about this particular opportunity. I shared many of their cautions and concerns, but I still sensed I should move ahead.

As I talked with them about it, my dad honored my heart, thoughts, and desires. He trusted that my heart wanted to do good. He trusted the Holy Spirit would help me make a wise decision, yet willingly shared his concerns for things he felt would lead me to regret.

Even though my dad was fully releasing me to make this decision, I continued to pursue his honest opinion and thoughts about which direction to move. Some of these conversations were hard and confusing. I desperately wanted to please my dad, yet I also sensed I should move forward into this opportunity.

One afternoon during this season of question, Dad stopped me as I passed through our family room, where he was sitting. He reminded me that he'd been thinking and praying hard about this situation and that he cared deeply about me and the results of whatever I would choose. His care meant the world to me. We talked a little about what we were both sensing. Then I reminded him how valuable his opinion was to me.

"I know it is," he said, "and that puts a lot of responsibility on me. I don't take that lightly."

Those words are the kind of language that makes a girl's heart feel safe, protected, and invincible—when a man, and a good one at that, takes responsibility and intercedes on behalf of her heart and life. This conversation reminded me that when I honor Dad's voice in my life, it often brings out his fatherly desire to protect, love, and call me to life.

When you feel God calling you in a certain direction or to a certain place, don't ignore that prompting. But don't use it as your ticket to dishonor those around you with the trump card of "God said" either. When God wants something to happen, it is far more about saying "yes" to His Spirit in the daily promptings of life than it is proving

> GOD WILL OFTEN USE THE VOICE OF OUR AUTHORITIES TO TEST OUR MOTIVES AND HELP CLARIFY OUR NEXT STEP.

to the world that this is His will. God will often use the voice of our authorities to test our motives and help clarify our next step.

I'm continually learning that when we voluntarily seek the counsel of our dads, we are sending a message of value for their voice within our free-will choices. We understand that we are not victims to anyone, but victors who have the opportunity to invite the perspective, ideas, and thoughts of our God-ordained authority.

HOW HONOR AFFECTS OUR DREAMS

Jackie Hill Perry wisely said, "It is my treatment of other image bearers that defines what I truly believe about myself."[6] How we define our own value will be how we define the value of another. Whenever we react to the actions and attitudes of our authorities, considering them not worthy of honor, it would serve us well to check into how we are defining our own value. Are we honoring others the way we would like to be honored?

I don't know about you, but I'm coming to realize how much I want others to honor me because they value me as a person and not because they value what I do for them. But, for years, I assumed this wasn't the case. I assumed I needed to be something to them. Do things in the right way. Benefit them in acceptable ways in order to be honored as valuable in their eyes. But I discovered it was my position as God's daughter—that unshakable, unconditional place of value—that actually teaches me to act in honorable ways and changes the way I define the value of others.

I have tried honoring my dad because I wanted to please him. If we are trying to honor so we can be pleasing to our dads, we will get exhausted. But if we are simply honoring the value of both the position and the person of our dads, honor becomes a little less complicated. Instead of striving to please, we seek to align ourselves with the value God has placed on us and them.

The story of Joseph in Genesis[7] gives us a clear picture of how our lives are affected when we know we are valued daughters and choose to value those around us through honor. Like Esther, Joseph was placed into God's mission because of his honor, not because he pushed for the dreams God had given him.

Joseph grew up in quite the family. He knew all about the good, the bad, and the ugly in family relationships. His brothers' lives were marked by comparison, envy, and having to bring others low in order to feel higher themselves. They knew clearly that they were *not* favored sons, so they continually worked to prove themselves and please their dad, while Joseph did so almost without trying. I don't believe it's right to have favorites. I have a lot of compassion for Joseph's brothers, because they weren't valued and loved like he was.

However, it's good for us to realize how differently people act when they believe they're valued. The way Joseph was treated versus his brothers, and the way he lived versus his brothers, tells us a lot about the power of knowing our identity as children.

Joseph acted with honor and integrity, as a loved son. His brothers, on the other hand, were fighting to be pleasing. Fighting to be seen and have their own mission validated. Joseph had a few dreams (the literal, nighttime kind) that threatened his brother's positions. This threat and their own games of comparison moved them to rash action—selling their little brother into slavery.

Even though Joseph was a victim to his brothers' wrong choices, he continued to bring his best to whatever setting he found himself in. He always made the leaders around him more successful when he was on the job. This is one of the marks of people who are committed to honor: they hold values that change their surroundings without being in charge. This demeanor was what inevitably made Joseph the guy who was continually given authority over others as he honored the authority over him.

The same word that was used for Esther and Jesus was used for Joseph: favor. But favor is no synonym to ease. If anyone was watching the story of Joseph and stopped at the part where he was tossed into prison for doing the right thing, they would have concluded that honor wasn't working for him. If you were Joseph and you believed honor helped things go well with you, wouldn't you start to think it was a spoof? The guy was sold into slavery and then thrown into prison. Hardly sounds like things were going well.

But Joseph didn't quit honoring or using the gifts and character he had to impact his surroundings. Even in prison, he was pulling out his best china dishes. He found favor and was soon running the place.

I can only imagine the battle. The daily choice to keep believing that his God wasn't against him. All his boyhood dreams were seemingly crushed. Dreams he knew (and probably second-guessed) God had given him. Dreams that were getting chipped and crushed in front of his eyes. But his demeanor in the prison seems to show he kept his heart open and didn't stop serving and honoring those around him. He didn't stop believing His God.

When his prison buddies, the baker and the butler, said they had no interpretations for their unsettling dreams, Joseph replied, "Do not interpretations belong to God? Please tell them to me" (Genesis 40:8, NKJV). The weight of those words strike me each time I read them. Dreams, of all things. Joseph was dealing with other people's dreams. Dreams were his thing. If he was thinking about his own dreams when he said those words, I can only imagine the twinge of pain that came with saying them.

None of the dreams God gave him were in sight from where Joseph was standing. If he tried to picture how they could happen, I highly doubt slavery and imprisonment were included in his ideas. When he said, "Interpretations belong to God," he must have seen the irony of the circumstances around him. But he not only believed God was in charge, he believed these men's dreams would come to pass, even when his own dreams hadn't yet. He kept believing God and keeping his heart open to what he wasn't seeing, even when it felt like nothing in life was fair, and when it looked like God was going back on His promises.

Psalm 105:19 says this about Joseph's time in prison: "Until the time that his word came to pass, the word of the Lord tested him" (NKJV). As I have watched the lives of people older than me, I often see a common thread in their stories. First, a vision, a calling, or a dream connected to their purpose and person. Then, a season that tests their motivations for these dreams and redirects what they think about themselves and God. And, often, this season of waiting and testing came through their authorities pausing their dreams, cautioning their ideas, speaking into their character, or advising them to wait. It's not fun. When you're in it, life feels like it's going all wrong and it's largely unfair.

But when we continue to keep our hearts open and honoring, particularly to the authorities who surround us, there is opportunity for God to unfold the next part of the story. When we choose to shut our hearts off from the people who aren't promoting us the way we want them to, we may miss the opportunities for growth and miracles.

When our authorities are not doing things our way, it's instinctive to close our hearts off to them. My mom has reminded me over and over how little this actually works. She tells me, "You can never shut off your heart to love in one relationship and expect to keep it open in any other relationship, including your relationship with God."

One of the best ways we can keep our hearts open and honorable is by taking responsibility for our emotions, words, and actions. These are the things we can choose to honor God with, even if circumstances are outside our control. People can and do hurt us. People can and will affect us. People can and will say things to us that give us an opportunity to believe lies about ourselves and God. But at the end of the day, what we choose to believe, and therefore do as a result, is entirely up to us. It is no one else's responsibility.

THE MORE RESPONSIBILITY WE TAKE FOR WHAT WE FEEL, SAY, AND DO, THE FREER WE WILL BE.

When we believe this, it stops us from simply reacting to what happens in life. It gives us the ability to take responsibility for ourselves and place ourselves completely under God's mission. This is the only way we will walk in real freedom. It may seem freeing to be a child without responsibility, always vulnerable to what everyone else decides to do or not to do. But then we would continually act as victims in our relationships. We would merely respond in them, instead of taking ownership of our own choices and placing our hearts under the guidance of the Holy Spirit.

The more responsibility we take for what we feel, say, and do, the freer we will be. Because then we can let God plant new attitudes, words, and actions within us instead of being a victim of everyone else's choices.

Sometimes terrible things happen to us, and we can do nothing about it. Clearly Joseph was a victim to the harmful lies, fears, and actions of others. He was continually put in choiceless situations. But he kept putting down his walls by remembering what he did have the power to choose: how he would conduct himself.

Eventually, Joseph had an opportunity to pay back his victimizers, if he wanted to. He did some testing. He set some boundaries. He cried some deep tears. And then he understood: God had redeemed the situations where he had been a victim and used them to move him into his dreams.

He understood that his victimizers had made bad choices, but they were not ultimately in charge of the outcome of his life. God was. And somehow, he knew that the only way to enter into the mission of God was to continually believe God and honor his ways when none of it made sense. He took responsibility for himself, even within another's irresponsible choices. He understood that God always makes a way for us to walk in honor, even when people around us are not.

HONOR IS OFTEN THE ATTITUDE THAT ENHANCES OUR VOICE.

I don't believe honor for others takes away our voice, invalidates our questions, or requires us to lose our opinions. In fact, honor is often the attitude that enhances our voice. Esther, Joseph, and Jesus all honored authority, and their influence ultimately exceeded that of the people who were technically in charge.

When we choose honor toward authority, it usually leads to more leadership and influence than if we tried to push for authority, dreams, or influence in the first place. Honor should create an environment like the Kingdom of God. It doesn't mean we can't have conversations, ask questions, create boundaries, or appeal for different ways of doing things. It just means we do so with the attitude of honor.

Are we willing to let our best dishes be chipped and used and broken? Esther prepared a feast for her king husband and the man who wanted to kill her people. Something tells me she set the feasting table with the best dishes in her royal cupboards. Jesus got out His dishes with His parents before He ever gave up His life for the whole world. Joseph served people with his good dishes whether he was in a palace or a prison. The way these people honored their authorities and the people around them invited God to move them into their own places of honor.

If your dad hasn't called your dreams to life, given wise counsel in your questions, or honored the value of your gifts, I'm deeply sorry. But I also have this word of comfort for you: if we believe in God, no person can thwart who we are or the unique purpose He has for us. Ask Joseph with the coat of many colors. He will remind you that no one can mess it up for you when your heart is believing God.

Your dreams, gifts, talents, and person are worth a great deal to God. He wants to call to life the unique ways He has designed you to be a vessel of His presence to others. He doesn't want your life story to be one that displays something pretty without living fully for what matters. What if you got the good dishes out of the cupboard today and used them to honor the people right around you? I have a feeling this list of people may include your dad.

ACTING INTENTIONALLY

What is something you value that you could honor your dad with? Maybe you value your time. Have you spent any intentionally with your dad lately? Maybe you value organization. Could this help your dad in any way?

Make a list of some things that make you come alive. What activities, relationships, tasks, and places make you thrive? Then ask yourself why you feel alive in these places. Is it because of the people group you're interacting with? The things you learn? The skills you get to use? The problems you get to solve? The relationships built?

As you think through these things, ask yourself how you can actively hone your passions to serve the people around you. How might the attitude of honor change the way you go about your interactions, tasks, talents, and dreaming? What is something you could do this week to serve others with your best dishes in everyday circumstances?

ASK YOURSELF

o How can I honor my dad's voice as I make lifestyle choices and pursue dreams?

o How can I take responsibility for my emotions and actions, instead of living in reaction to my dad's choices and how he may trigger my emotions?

o Am I honoring my dad in order to please him, or am I honoring him because of the value God places on his position and person?

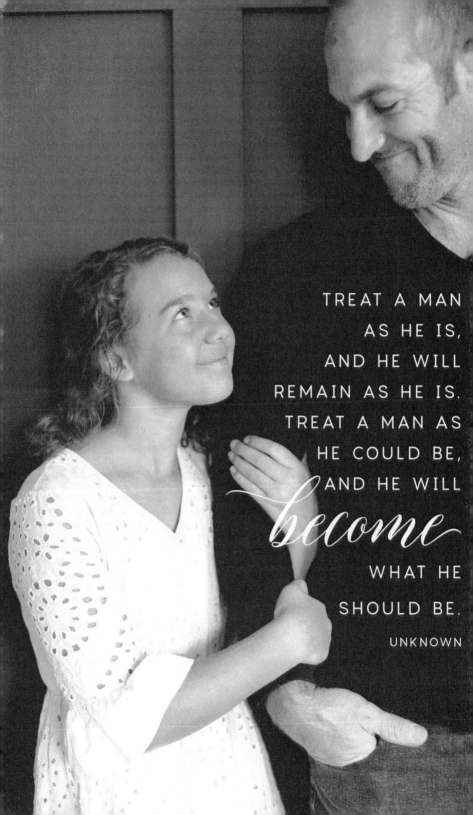

TREAT A MAN
AS HE IS,
AND HE WILL
REMAIN AS HE IS.
TREAT A MAN AS
HE COULD BE,
AND HE WILL
become
WHAT HE
SHOULD BE.
UNKNOWN

CHAPTER 7

hero

HONORING OUR DADS
EVEN WHEN WE DISAGREE WITH THEM

Every film watched, book read, or story told needs some form of hero. Where there's a problem, and every story has one, there is a hopeful anticipation for rescue, redemption, and change. It's been written a hundred different ways, but we keep being mesmerized by characters fighting through pain and obstacles to finally be rescued in heroic endings. We flock to hear speakers who have "an amazing story," we stand in line at the theater, and we recommend books that we couldn't put down. We are wired to love the pattern of a compelling story with an epic conclusion.

If you know the gospel, then you know why this story pattern matters. We're wired to love this pattern because it's the tale of the larger story of God. We need someone who sees and notices enough to step in and rescue us when all the odds are against us. We want a good guy and a bad guy, and we always hope someone worthy will win in the end.

For us girls, often the first hero of our story is Dad. Through a little girl's vision, dads seem heroically strong, protective, and courageous. We are cutely enamored with them. Like the days when my dad's tickles, affection, and strength put me under a bit of a love spell. Our delight with each other was simple. I remember the nights he would sit on the edge of my bed and pray for me before I fell asleep. That was extra fun on no-shave Saturdays. My texture-loving palms would feel his scruff as he'd lean over me and talk about the day. He still does that sometimes, and I still place my cupped palm on his beard. In moments like this, he's easily the best guy in the world.

Some stages are easy. Some days, dads seem like the hero of the story. On those days it's easy to honor them. But then there are those other kinds of days and stages. The kinds with delicate combinations of misunderstandings, losses, triggered pain, hormones, disappointments, and spilled milk. It's on those days that dads seem to be a far cry from the hero of the story. Because heroes are strong and manly, have nice hair and capes, and probably don't tell lame jokes, right?

It doesn't take long before little girls envision their hero as the phantom boy of their dreams. But even with that natural switch of interest, deep down we still long for our dads to be our heroes. Opposingly, the stories we hear in real life, on the Hallmark Channel, or in novels don't often cast Dad as the hero but the villain. Dad is the guy who causes our problems, keeps us from our dreams, and makes life difficult.

In our own lives, we sometimes also see our dad as the villain who is causing our problems, keeping us from our dreams, and making life difficult. Some of the things that rip off our dads' capes are simple—personality differences (or sometimes worse, similarities), opposite love languages,[1] or habits that tap dance on nerves. These things create real issues in getting the love that is in us to be obvious and felt by our dads. They are also the things that can make it complicated to receive love from our dads, when they may not know how to express love in a way that speaks to how we're wired.

But then there is another set of things that tears off capes and ties black masks to our dads' faces. They aren't the trivial, everyday things. They are things like sin, opposing values, counter-opinions on what it means to succeed, or different interpretations of God's Word. These things make us wonder how to honor our fathers while still addressing things that shouldn't go on, sticking to the values we think are important, and allowing ourselves room to think. In order to work through these hard differences, we may need to ask intentional questions to understand how to honor our dads even when we disagree with them.

GOOD QUESTIONS

Questions are like the chamomile tea of conversations. I like a cup before bed, though I don't always take time for it. When I do, it sets the mood for rest. It reminds me to settle down and turn on a slower mode then I had in my hurried day.

Questions can do this in disagreeable conversations. They disarm the armed and dangerous. They give a platform for the quieter voices and settle the ones who won't stop talking long enough to understand their own words. They can relax tension and help us or others turn on a different mode.

I have a theory that we should automatically switch to old English accents whenever we start to disagree with someone. Or really any accent other than our own. Think about it. It would make us slow down our words, think about what we're saying, and probably create laughter as we say it. Plus, burning someone in an English accent just seems more potent and classy.

But since no one has found this theory successful (being that no one has actually tried it), I return to a more practical option: questions. I hope these questions slow down the conversation and add some good taste to our words. More than anything, good questions can help put down the guard of the person we're disagreeing with. Questions imply that we want their thoughts to be heard. We value what they're bringing to the conversation. Questions suggest that we're open to reason and that we're not coming with predetermined ideas, conclusions, or agendas.

In everyday discussions, I often forget to ask questions intentionally. I'm quicker to state my own thoughts before I consider another's. But I'm learning a well-placed question can help turn the conversation in a healthy direction. From time to time, I also need to ask *myself* some questions to understand what I may be dealing with in a disagreement. Most of the questions we'll be talking about are not something I premeditated in a real-life discussion, but later on

I understood they could have been helpful. Others came not from my own relationship with my dad but from watching others walk through differences. These questions are not a list to carry around or try to remember. I'm simply stating them here to get us thinking about how we can understand ourselves or our dads in a new way.

QUESTION 1

Am I disagreeing with my dad because of the actual subject, or am I reacting to the way this conversation makes me feel?
Sometimes we dub our fathers unworthy of honor because of how we feel. I'm learning not to let emotions control my honor. It's good for me to remind myself that while my dad can say and do things that step on my own sensitivities, he does not have control over my emotions. And I don't want my emotions to have control over me, either. Instead, they can remind me to check what I am letting myself be controlled by: lies, my flesh, or the Spirit of truth.

Sometimes it's helpful to voice what we're feeling in a disagreement instead of going in circles about the subject itself. I remember once when my mom voiced a concern about something one of my siblings was doing. My sibling was just headed out the door to spend time with friends when my mom mentioned the concern. It was bad timing to try and address this issue. My sibling instantly reacted. But instead of just telling my mom that they disagreed with her concern, my sibling said, "Your comment makes me feel judged and misunderstood, Mom. I'm not trying to do anything wrong by choosing this."

> I'M LEARNING NOT TO LET EMOTIONS CONTROL MY HONOR.

Once my sibling returned home, my parents were able to have an understanding conversation about the concern. They were all on the same page once they talked about it. My sibling was smart to name what they felt—judged and misunderstood—as the problem, instead of making a big deal about the concern itself. It could have turned into a heated disagreement if they hadn't recognized the real issue.

Sometimes we are quick to assume that we are disagreeing about the subject at hand when, really, we're disagreeing because we don't like the way our dad is stepping on personal sensitivities. This can make us feel unloved, judged, misunderstood, or unheard. Disagreeing can be a tool we use to protect ourselves from feeling what we don't want to feel.

We can often bring clarity to a disagreement by saying things like "When you say this, I feel misunderstood," or "When you do that it comes across like my opinion doesn't matter in this conversation."

Sometimes it takes a while to realize what the point of disagreement even is. It's like we're on a merry-go-round, going in circles so fast all we can think about is keeping our vomit down. Meanwhile, we're completely missing the point of the conversation.

For my dad and me, most of our disagreements aren't disagreements at all. They are feelings within a conversation that make us assume we're on different pages. The disagreement is essentially the tool we use to protect ourselves from things we don't want to feel. Inwardly we're saying, *If I'm right and he is wrong, then I won't feel this way.* So we use different terminology or come from a different angle, trying to make a point. All the while we're nearly on the same page, but we can't tell because we have different feelings about it.

When you name a feeling in a conversation, I encourage you to stay away from the phrase "You make me feel" and stick to "When you do this or say this, I feel this." There can be different reasons we feel what we feel. But it's important to remember that no one can control our feelings. They can, however, trigger a lie we're already believing.

Have you ever reacted on a level ten, when the subject in discussion was a casual level two? That's a good indicator that you're feeling lie-based emotion that has nothing to do with the current situation. The current situation triggered it, but it's not the reason for your strong emotions.

When I deal with the lie-based feelings in a given situation, I often wake up to the realization that I can actually agree with my dad. I just didn't think I could because of the feelings involved in the disagreement.

When we name what we're feeling, it's not to create a hypersensitive environment or blame others, but to communicate what's going on inside us. This may keep us from disagreeing about things we actually agree about.

QUESTION 2
Is this worth the battle?

Sometimes I hear my mom friends use the phrase "choose your battles." They say it when their kid has done about twenty-five consecutive naughty things. They've learned the difference between their kid just being a kid and their kid being rebellious. They don't battle every little thing, or their kid and their sanity would need to be checked into a recovery home.

This parenting tip, "choose your battles," is also a good tip for us as daughters. Are all these differences worth battling over? Some differences are worth laying down simply out of honor for our dad, even if we disagree with him. But other times it's truly important to pursue a middle ground.

There are things I do today simply to honor my dad, not because I personally feel convicted about them. But those few things are not a burden to me. I hardly think of them. There will always be these measures of honor to hold in our lives. We don't live on an island by ourselves. The choice to honor even when we disagree is not reserved only for our dads. If I don't get this idea of honor with my dad, I often face the same differences with other authorities, or even with my siblings or friends. We were not created to do everything we think is best. We were created for relationships in which we will often do something contrary to our personal style, way, or ideas to honor others.

So how do we know when to do things the way our dads prefer and when to appeal to our own preferences, convictions, and ideas?

In Romans 14, Paul talks about what to do when we have minor differences with other people. The Romans were dealing with things like what kinds of meat to eat or not eat and which days to honor or not honor. They were toying with differing standards in their lives.

Paul's solution was simple: live before God in personal faith. Then be willing to honor another person's idea, value, or boundary, even if you don't agree with it. When you disagree with your dad about a principle that God has left open for each person to individually discern, it may be time to defer to the principle God has made clear: honor.

Because there is freedom of choice, you are free to make your own decisions and form your own convictions. I don't believe honor means you have to live exactly like your dad does or take on all his convictions for yourself. But you can make conscious decisions to honor your dad's convictions in ways God's Word and Spirit direct you.

Honoring your dad's preferences, convictions, or ideas might look different in different stages of your life. Ask yourself, how can I honor my dad in my current stage, even if we disagree? Do I need to set aside any of my preferences for a season? This does not mean you have to hold all his convictions, but it could mean choosing to practice something important to him while you live in his household.

There are things God has made clear in Scripture that are not up to our personal conviction. If God clearly states something is sin, we should stand on that truth whether our dad agrees or not (although we should do it in the character and fruit of the Spirit). Choose your battles, and learn what is scriptural in your situation. Is the issue at hand one that could be interpreted several different ways? Is it contradictory to the gospel and God's clear morals? Is this a time to simply honor instead of pushing for what you would personally do? Answering this may help you know how to frame your mind for the conversations and decisions surrounding differences.

When you're not sure what you should do about a difference between you and your dad, ask yourself if it's worth the battle. Be willing to do some things that are different than what you would personally choose, simply to honor your dad. But then also be willing to follow Jesus into new things you haven't done or tried before, knowing He will give you wisdom to know how to maintain honor in a new choice. Whatever decision you make, make it in the fear of God, not fear of your dad, and out of love for God, not love for what feels comfortable.

QUESTION 3

What is your target?

Sometimes we need to ask our parents why they believe what they believe. Why are they teaching us this? Hoping that for us? Recommending this or keeping us from that? We need to find out what they're aiming at. Because sometimes we both have the same target, we're simply approaching the target from two different angles.

Have you ever been presented with an opportunity that your father wasn't sure about? I have. It can be hard to know what to do, especially if you feel the Lord is asking you to take steps of faith in that direction.

My dad and I share nearly all the same values and vision for the world. We read the Word through the same lens and want to follow Jesus with the same abandon. But we are distinct personalities and have had different opinions about how to carry out these values and visions sometimes.

However, I don't know the complication of being on a vastly different page from my dad, but I've had people around me who do. So I'll attempt to speak about how I've watched them put capes back on their dads.

Here are a few things I suggest. First, ask your authorities' advice and listen. God's Word makes it clear that the counsel of our parents is something to be taken seriously. If their reasoning or values don't line up with how you interpret God's Word, ask more questions. Sometimes, at face value, their opinions may feel "stuck" in some way of thinking that you want to be free from. Ask questions to understand the heart behind their value.

For instance, they may feel uncomfortable with you going to a different church than the one you grew up in. You know you have valid reasons to leave this church. But before you do, ask them about the things they value in their church. What made them choose this church in the first place?

Let's say they told you that they chose this church because they sang hymns instead of modern worship songs. If you don't understand why you value this, ask more questions. "What is it about hymns that you value?"

They'll probably give you reasons like "good doctrine instead of emotionalism." Meanwhile, you may feel like their church lacks some vibrance, and you'd be up for some emotion here and there.

This would be a good time to ask more questions, such as, "What are some of the false doctrines you see in modern worship songs?"

Asking these kinds of questions does a few things. For one, it puts down their guards. You're not here to fight, you're here to understand. And it helps you maintain honor even when you disagree. It also gives you an opportunity to learn. Sometimes we assume a tradition, opinion, or way of thinking is wrong because of the way we've seen it played out. We may be right. They may have some unbiblical ways of thinking or operating. But we at least want to give them an opportunity to be understood. They may have some valuable targets we should aim at if we begin to understand them.

When we ask questions, we find out what our parents are aiming at with their actions, choices, and principles. Through these questions, you may discover there is more truth to their opinion than you gave it credit for. And listening may keep you from figuring that out the hard way.

Once you understand what they're aiming at, look for ways to honor that target, even if you don't agree with the specific way they approach it. For instance, their goal in keeping you at their church may turn out to be about maintaining good doctrine. That's a good goal. Maybe you see other ways to carry this out, but at least voice your value for this goal and talk to them about how you hope to maintain it even if you choose to go to another church.

Now I know that sometimes you can't agree with your dad's target in the first place. If so, ask yourself this question.

QUESTION 4

Am I disagreeing with God's Word or my dad's word?

Sometimes parents teach their children things as though they are the Word of God, when they're not. Other times, parents teach their children things that *are* in the Word of God, but they teach it in a way that cuts off the heart of their child. In this situation, it's easy for the child to reject God's Word because of the way it was taught to them.

I'm here to prod you to search for yourself. Read His Word and take it seriously, no matter how your parents taught it to you or how your friends or church, new or old, interpret it. Ask the Spirit for personal revelation on how to follow Jesus amid differences. Then ask yourself, *whose words am I truly disagreeing with? My parent's or God's?*

It's good to remember that even if good ideas from the Word of God were taught to us in bad ways, that doesn't keep them from being good ideas. That's like assuming we hate squash because we didn't like the way our mom prepared it. It may not be our favorite, but, at the very least, let's be open to the possibility that not all squash is soggy and tasteless. Made well, there may be something wonderful we haven't tasted yet.

If a principle from the Word of God was taught to you in a way that made it become a bondage instead of a blessing, then it is healthy to deal with this bondage before God. Miraculously, this same principle can be a blessing in your life when you embrace it in freedom. Don't reject truth that will set you free in an attempt to free yourself from a misconception that caused bondage. God's Word contains the ways of true freedom and life.

QUESTION 5
What would you love to see your daughter do?

A few years ago, I was looking into attending several different training programs and Bible schools. There were a few things I wanted to learn and a few places I felt drawn to go. At the time, I couldn't quite tell if it was the Spirit of God nudging me in those directions or if it was my own discontentment with my current stage of life.

I began having conversations with my dad about these different opportunities. My dad, for reasons I didn't understand, felt frustrated by these conversations. I began getting frustrated too. Why did it feel like we were limiting each other instead of understanding each other? My dad didn't have a problem with what I wanted to do, just with the timing and finances involved. Sometimes my dad's cautions made total sense to me and I was grateful for objective feedback as I made decisions. Other times, his cautions felt more personal and difficult to receive.

Finally, one day I walked into his office and asked, "Dad, what would you love to see me do this next year? If you could imagine what would be best for your daughter, what would that be?" I was surprised by how vulnerable this question felt. It was safer not to know, in a way. Then I wouldn't have to face what his desires were, especially when I was confused about my own. But in another sense, I was surprised I hadn't asked this question sooner. Why had I assumed I knew what he wanted, and reacted based on that assumption, instead of asking him to freely share?

He didn't answer right away, but he told me he'd think about it. A few days later, we sat down to have another conversation about it. He talked to me about his desire for me to be fully alive and do what I felt called to do. But then he was able to honestly share some of what he sensed about why I wanted to do these things.

I was in a season of searching, and for some reason these programs and places looked like they would help me figure out who I was and where I wanted to go. I'm sure they could have helped, but my motivations for being drawn to them were unhealthy attempts to define who I was. Dad sensed this before I could. Once I understood this more clearly, I realized this wasn't the best time to pursue those goals. Even if they came later, God wanted me right where I was for now.

Dad came to me several times after I asked this question and thanked me for asking it. It helped him understand what was going on inside him and how he could better advise me. It switched on his fatherly instincts to love, support, and protect. It made him feel like his voice was honored, not just tolerated, in this situation.

Even if your dad doesn't respond well to this question, keep his cape on by seeking his blessing. If you feel led to do something he wouldn't prefer, explain your heart for why you desire to do it. Then, ask if he could bless the decision, even if it isn't his preference. This alone will show that you value his voice and opinion. Some dads won't use vocabulary like "I bless you to do this" or "I bless you to go here," but at the very least, seek out some kind of conversation to get his blessing and counsel on your dreams, goals, and lifestyle choices. He may not have perfect words for it, but seek it.

SEEKING COMMUNITY

Whether your differences with your dad are minor or major, God does not expect you to figure everything out for yourself. Instead, God designed us to walk with people through our big questions.

When it comes to connecting with others about our questions, we often think it should be obvious that we are struggling, and we hope someone reaches out to us. Or sometimes the opposite happens: we fear someone will reach out, and we're not sure we want to expose what's going on. No matter the case, we need to be willing to initiate. Ask someone out for coffee. Pull them aside after church. Reach out to people who can help you navigate your situation in honor.

Within community, growth happens when we are honest and don't try to save face. It's vital to have people in your life you can share openly with if you're struggling with your dad. However, choose these people wisely. A counselor or your pastor's wife are often neutral people you can be open with. Seek out people who are there to help you, not necessarily to fix your dad.

Many of us young women have yet to tap into the power of mentorship. We tend to surround ourselves with friends who make us feel good. Of course, there's indispensable value in healthy friendships with people our age. But we should also be pursuing connection with people who have already experienced the parts of life we're facing for the first time. If we're dealing with complications in how to relate to, coincide with, or honorably disagree with our dad, we need people to help us navigate the conversations, decisions, and steps needed to walk in honor.

If you truly don't have people around who are trustworthy, pray. Pray that God would send people into your life to counsel you through your questions and decisions. Every girl needs people she can be honest and open with. But remember, mentors in our lives are only there to point us to Jesus, not to ultimately answer our questions.

Recently a wise woman I know was telling me about some hard decisions she had to make in order to live out the true gospel. Her dad disagreed with her about these decisions. She had mentors and people around her who were discipling her, yet, when it came down to the final decisions, she sensed strongly that she needed to simply hear from the Spirit of God on what to do.

She said, "I could have asked my youth group friends what they would do, but, instead, I just got on my knees and said, 'Father, I have no idea what I'm doing. I'm just a girl, and I don't know how to handle this. Would you teach me how to think? How would you like me to honor my dad?'" One step at a time, He gave her the answers through His Word and His still, small voice. A personal relationship with God and His Word will ultimately be the best way to help you know what steps to take.

If your parents' mission cannot align with God's, I pray He will give you wisdom to know how to honor and trust Him as you make decisions about this reality. His Spirit can and will guide you as you surrender to His mission.

The Father wants to walk with you personally, and He wants to walk with you through other people's presence and guidance in your life. He has abundant good in mind for you, even in the complications surrounding differences, and the resulting decisions that come with them. He will be most gentle as you bring your raw uncertainty into His presence.

> HEROES OFTEN HAVE GRAY HAIR AND BAD JOKES, NOT SUPERPOWERS AND BILLOWING CAPES.

Whatever questions you have for yourself or your dad today, I pray they will help your heart draw out the hero in your dad. Our dads are often more heroic than we give them credit for. Sometimes it simply takes a mindset shift for us to recognize the daily sacrifices they make for us, the lifelong benefits we will have because they provided for us, and the time they invested into loving and teaching us. I'm finding real heroes often have gray hair and bad jokes, not superpowers and billowing capes.

ACTING INTENTIONALLY

Consider asking your dad about his experiences with his own dad. Did he ever disagree with his dad? How did he handle the disagreement? What did he do to honor his dad? Does he have regrets, or has he seen benefits from heeding his dad's cautions and advice?

What does your dad think about honor? What one dad feels honored by, another may be annoyed by. As you work through differences or interact in daily life, learn to honor your dad in a way that fits his personal style, generation, and ideas.

ASK YOURSELF

○ What question could I ask my dad to draw out the heart behind his values?

○ How can I practice naming emotions in conversations instead of letting emotions control conversations?

○ How can I thank my dad for the ways he has acted as a hero in my life?

IN FACT, IT'S IN THE IMPERFECT—
THE DIRT—WHERE THINGS

grow.

NOT DESPITE THE MESS
AND TENSION, BUT RIGHT SMACK
IN THE MIDDLE OF IT.

LARA CASEY[1]

CHAPTER 8

growth

MOVING PAST AVOIDING BAD
INTO PLANTING GOOD

I pace when I talk on the phone and use hand gestures akin to those of my childhood choir director. (Clearly, this helps the person on the other end understand me better.) I was doing both as I talked with my dad on a Friday afternoon in August. I walked from the kitchen table where I was working to the entryway door, then back to the table, then to the kitchen sink, and again into the entryway, conducting with commitment. Our family was about to release a new album, and that Friday was the deadline for the graphic design to be finished up.

It's my job to work with the designer, and I like the work. But deadlines and pressure are not my sweet spot. As working hours were coming to a close, Dad called to ask for another photo to be inserted on an inside page. I didn't like the idea. Besides, I was dealing with deadlines, the opinions of about nine people and their mother, and the varied tastes of several generations. This spot, my friend, is where Deborah usually gets uglier than cheap mascara on the hottest day of July.

What is your spot? The place where some everyday difference brings out something less than your normal, angelic self?

Each of us will bring our own personality and dispositions into our relationships. When we mingle lies and fears with these things, we create a personal collection of ugly reactions. Some are loud and obvious. Others are quiet and stuffed. Some bring up conflict. Others avoid it. We will each have our sensitive spots, which then create sensitive spots in our relationships.

Often these sensitive spots have nothing to do with the Bible, the gospel, worldview, lifestyle choices, theology, or if Melchizedek[2] was a Christophany or a regular priest in a royal robe. Basically, spots where there is no measuring unit for right or wrong, no commentaries or hard facts, just our own opinion standing in the far corner of the boxing ring, facing our dad's. These differences can happen anywhere, on any old day, for any reason at all, including reasons we hardly know how to explain. Relationships are anything but explainable or straightforward. It takes time, lessons, and humility to learn to love our people well.

> IT TAKES TIME,
> LESSONS, AND
> HUMILITY TO
> LEARN TO
> LOVE OUR
> PEOPLE WELL.

On that Friday in August, I had an opportunity to practice what God had been teaching me about honor. I felt tension rising in my body as Dad told me about an office meeting in which the staff had suggested that some album details be changed. I asked him a series of questions, attempting to understand why this last-minute change was important to him. His answers to my questions kept confirming how much I disagreed with him.

I asked myself, *Is this a time to set a boundary?* I had been doing the legwork for this project. I had attempted to hear everyone's opinions and ideas, and had found a middle ground I thought would make most family members and office staff happy. And I didn't like my dad's idea. His reasoning felt a little old-fashioned and unimportant to me. Should I just tell him it was too late and we were going to leave it how it was?

I felt a nudge from the Spirit saying this wasn't the honorable response for this moment. I had a passing thought that I shouldn't disregard my dad's suggestion, even if I would have had a right to do so. I continued to ask him more questions to see if we were misunderstanding each other.

Nope. The more he talked, the less I agreed.

I asked myself if there was time to make this change. It was clear to me that if this was a change *I* wanted, I would find time for it. I knew it was time to treat my dad's opinion with the same honor I'd want my opinion to be treated with. "Okay, Dad," I said. "For some reason I'm not able to track with your way of thinking or understand why this is important. But if you feel it is, I'll make it happen. What do I need to do first?"

I felt the tension drain from my body. Somehow, I keep forgetting how freeing God's ways are. Sure, I would have had the right to keep pushing my point. But how free would my soul have been? Would we have experienced peace in our conversation? What kind of seed would I have been planting?

My dad said something kind. It was as though my saying those words, and choosing honor, released us both to *feel* the honor. I could hear his voice come alive on the other end of the phone, and I instantly felt honored in return.

Dad texted and emailed me a few times the rest of the day and kept reinforcing thanks for what I was doing and praising how "awesome" I was. It struck me as funny. It's like honor is the language of parents. It turns on some other kind of mode that makes them want to douse us in love. Of course, if I had decided to say it was too late for this change, my dad would still have been responsible to respect my role and love me. But when we walk in the Spirit, we walk beyond our duties, inviting each other to natural, healthy ways of relating that bubble over from our hearts.

That Friday was my invitation to plant honor. You, with your different personality, story, and dad, may receive an entirely different invitation. You may be one of those people who sits still, talks quietly, and looks cute as you talk on the phone (perhaps with an occasional roll of the eyes). For you, the invitation may be to voice your opinion instead of going with what everyone else wants while inwardly resenting yourself or them for it.

If we assume that honor always means letting go of our opinion or always doing what our dad prefers, we may be missing the whole point. Inward control and stuffing emotions can be rooted in the same rebellion as not being willing to lay down our opinion. Because inwardly, when we don't think God created us with a credible voice, we are not walking in truth, and often we silently sow seeds of bitterness, self-protection, or resentment. It's still not honor. And usually the people around us can feel that.

Honor can say, "I'd like to try this," or "Why don't we do it this way?" because this may be what it takes to be ruled by the Holy Spirit instead of shutting down, shutting others out, or performing for them in a victim attitude that dishonors them inwardly. Sometimes the honorable choice is explaining our point more clearly, because it may help our dad understand something helpful about us or the situation. The attitude of honor can be honest about an opinion instead of just going with everyone else's opinion. Our honor is not measured by our words or actions, but by how much those words and actions are aligned with the Spirit of truth.

When my dad got home after that whirlwind Friday, he hugged me and then said, "Today was a tough day for me. I had a lot on my plate. But the way you responded to and handled my requests was a gift in my day." Then he added, "I know, at one point, you would have handled a situation like this differently."

Thanks, Dad. Just when I thought I was the heroine, I was reminded of my weakness without the power of the Holy Spirit. Just weeks before, we'd had another discussion about the design work, which went quite differently. We'd argued about it in ways that were less than peaceful and kind—I threw out harsh glances, exaggerated points, and angry tones. Dad later apologized for handling the situation poorly, but I was just as much of a role player.

Even as a child, I could use my words and intensity to win in any given conversation. I often played the role of the lawyer-kid who could leave my defendant speechless and a little wounded. I don't like this about myself, and I've had to deal with shadowing shame for how intense I can be.

But can we just have a gospel choir "hallelujah" for the reality that we never have to be bound to anything that isn't true about who we are in Christ? I can trade intensity for healthy passion. And word knives for good communication. I guess what I said earlier isn't true. Maybe these issues have everything to do with the Bible, the gospel, worldview, lifestyle choices, theology, and Christ who is after the order of Melchizedek—a royal Priest making up His royal priesthood of measly little me and you.

We're in the beautiful work of aligning ourselves with the truth of our Cross-redeemed identities. In this identity, we have a voice and value. Our opinions and thoughts are a needed element in our relationships. But in this identity, we also have the freedom to honor others' opinions and willingly lay down our thoughts and ideas for them, as Christ did for us. As we continue to align our own hearts with these truths, the Holy Spirit gives us daily wisdom for how to plant seeds of honor in our unique relationships.

PLANTING SEEDS

In our everyday differences, interactions, and conversations, we affect the people around us. If we're not intentional, we often let interactions pass by without seeing the ways we could have planted good seeds in our relationships.

We can never successfully control or change people, but we can affect their lives by the seeds we plant within our interactions and within our prayers. Planting a seed takes intention. It means preparing the ground of our garden, knowing when to plant so the seed will flourish, and intentionally watering and tending before we see results.

That's the kind of work we want to talk about next. Intentional planting. The seeds we will use to grow our garden are seeds that come from the life of Christ inside us. People can taste His fruit in our lives through our attitudes, actions, and words.

As we talk about planting seeds, there are a few things to keep in mind. Our job is to tend the life of Christ inside us, so others can tangibly know Him through us. We need to start with good seeds in order for good things to grow. We cannot cause the growth or guarantee the harvest, but we can faithfully tend through every season. We cannot make our dad, ourselves, or our relationships what we imagine them to be. But we can plant seeds, water them, and watchfully tend to their needs. Then we surrender the harvest to Christ.

If your dad is not tending his own garden well, don't try to manipulate his growth. Work on your own. No matter how he responds, you will still reap the blessings from what you're intentionally sowing.

> IF YOUR DAD IS NOT TENDING HIS OWN GARDEN WELL, DON'T TRY TO MANIPULATE HIS GROWTH.

You always reap more than you sow. Anything you put in the ground in faith becomes abundantly more than it was in its original state. What feels tedious and hard to tend today will nearly be forgotten when you're tasting the results of growth.

Before we move into a conversation about seeds we can plant, I want to acknowledge the power of the seeds our dads did or didn't plant in our lives. One of the seeds that affects our lives the most is the words our dads use. Let's talk a little about why God created us to listen closely to the words of our dads.

SEEDS YOUR DAD HAS OR HASN'T SOWN INTO YOUR LIFE

These days, my sweet dad is overflowing with compliments and kind words (and a strong dose of teasing). But Dad wasn't always so free with his loving words. He has used words that have hurt or shut me down. Other times, silence stood in the place of any words at all. And sometimes the absence of loving words hurts as much as the presence of hurtful words. Positive, negative, and absent words have all had an effect on my life. I'm guessing you could say the same.

We seem to form our internal identity around what our dads say or don't say about us and to us. I remember how, on my sixteenth birthday, my dad read a blessing over me. He named gifts he saw in me, blessed my strengths, and affirmed the ways I used my talents.

I remember hearing the blessing and honestly thinking my dad didn't know me as well as I thought he did. When he named some of my gifts and strengths, I thought he was off just a hair. I had taken tests to help me understand my spiritual gifts and personality and apparently forgot to inform him of the results. All the same, I was grateful for his kind words and blessing.

Fast forward nearly a decade. A friend of mine stumbled onto an old video of my dad sharing that blessing with me on my birthday. We had just been talking about callings, passions, interests, and trying to navigate what God has for us in life. After watching the video, my friend messaged me and said, "Deborah, everything your dad spoke to you when you were sixteen is exactly what you've been talking about."

What? I thought I remembered it being a little "off" from who I wanted to be. So I watched the clip too. My friend was right. Since my sixteenth birthday, I had involved myself in a broad range of activities, ministry adventures, friendships, and people groups. I'd used my talents and gifts in a variety of ways. But now I was in my twenties and finally finding some things that stuck and felt in alignment with who God created me to be. Many things I had tried seemed to be falling by the wayside. But the activities, motivations, talents, gifts, and passions that stuck were nearly verbatim what my dad had spoken over me.

We often live out what our fathers have spoken over us. I wonder if this is why Jesus didn't start His ministry until He heard those words of affirmation from His Father: "This is my beloved Son in whom I am well pleased" (Matthew 3:17). Those words were tied to the Spirit of God bringing power into His life to do what He was purposed to do here on earth.

The good seeds our dads plant with their words grow purpose and life inside us. A father's words invite his daughter's imagination to connect to who God created her to be. A father breathes life into the part of his daughter's heart that dreams, creates, applies herself to daily tasks, learns, and achieves. The way a dad talks to his girl when she shows him her art project, plays piano, tries out for a team, or completes a task gives her signals for what she is capable of and how she could try harder. This helps to shape a daughter's interests, her calling, who she is, and what makes her come alive.

When my dad speaks on family life, he talks a lot about the weight of a father's words in the life of his children. At the end of these sermons, he usually invites all the families present to come to the front of the room. They cluster close together, looking a little curious about what Dad is going to ask them to do. He then explains that he wants them to practice speaking words of life and blessing to each other, right there on the spot. It starts with husbands to wives, then wives to husbands, then parents to children, then children to each other.

I have watched this transpire in many churches and communities, and I've seen sad and beautiful things happen. There's rarely any session like this that doesn't include tears. But what always surprises me is the tears in the youngest of children. Children hardly old enough to fully comprehend what's happening. Three- and four-year-olds will weep in the arms of their father as he speaks kindly to them. It seems words, even if they don't fully understand them, reach a deep place inside and pull up formerly unexpressed emotions. I have also seen teenagers and adults from godly homes cry deeply as they hear affirmation about who they are, and receive blessings over the purposes of God for their lives. Sometimes we forget to speak the things we value about the people closest to us. Sometimes, even if we come from good homes, words of life and affirmation just aren't voiced often enough.

I want to give deep understanding to the loss of not hearing affirming words from your dad. If your dad's words have been more like choking thorns instead of life-producing seeds, this is a loss. A father's words affect a daughter deeply. Sometimes so deeply it surprises me. But this need for life-giving words is intense on purpose. We were created to build our lives and identities around the words of Father God, and this earthly relationship with our dads helps us understand how God wants to speak to us.

As much as we naturally form our identity around the words of our fathers, this doesn't mean we are limited by their lack of words or that we have to live out their negative ones. Our dads' words don't ultimately form our destiny. What we believe does. The impact of our dads' words gives us a picture of what it's like to form our lives around the voice of our Father God. It's reminding us to live our lives centered around who God is and what God says about us, instead of trying to form our identities around what we do or what the world says is noble and good.

When dads talk to us throughout our days, they show us something personal about our God. My dad randomly hugs me and tells me I'm beautiful or a real blessing multiple times a day. He pats me on the shoulder and tells me, "You've got this." He kisses me on the cheek and tells me he loves me before I go to bed at night. He checks in to see how my day is going. He takes time to tell me a story or a joke he knows I'll get a kick out of. He gives me caution or advice for how to handle a situation or change an attitude. He makes sure to let me know when I've done something well or he sees me growing. There are often tears in his eyes as he talks to me about how much I mean to him and how proud he is of me. This happens throughout my everyday activities, and it also happens in intentional, set-aside time to communicate and seek his counsel.

This is how God wants to speak to us. Throughout our days, as we go to bed and wake up. And in the time we set aside to be with Him and seek Him in intentional prayer and time in His Word. He wants to give wings to the unique dreams and desires of our hearts. He wants to enjoy us, encourage us, and talk to us about His simple delight in who we are.

If your dad hasn't planted good seeds with his words in your life, you still have an opportunity to know a God who wants to. Because of the authority of the shed blood of Jesus, any negative words spoken to you can be rendered powerless when you renounce them and step into the truth of what God speaks over your life.

A friend of mine once talked with me about what she does when her father speaks negative words to her. She goes to a private place and brings the words her dad spoke into the presence of God. Then she seeks His heart for what is true.

Maybe you need to take some time today to think about the words your dad has or hasn't spoken to you. Are there words of criticism, shame, or condemnation to bring before God? What did those words cause you to believe about God or yourself? Bring them into the presence of God and allow Him to reveal His nature and speak His words to your heart. His words will be the seeds that grow life and purpose for all the activity and actions we choose in life. As we receive His words over our lives, the resulting harvest will give us fresh seeds to do some of our own planting.

PLANTING SEEDS IN YOUR DAD'S LIFE

On my way to work this morning, rain pattered on my windshield, Shane and Shane sang a psalm through my stereo system, and the words of Jonathan Edwards ran through my mind. I said them aloud as a prayer. "Lord, stamp eternity on my eyeballs."[3]

I live differently when I live through the lens of eternity. I began to picture how the scenes of my day might play out differently if I saw my actions and inter-actions from an eternal vantage point. I replayed my morning meeting with my mom in my head. If I had been more aware of eter-nity, the little frustra-tions that came up in the meeting wouldn't have mattered half as much. I pictured walking into the office and greeting our secretaries. My heart flooded with a different level of love and honor for them. I pictured working with my dad throughout the day. Instinctively, I knew I wanted to be kinder, more relatable, and vis-ibly loving.

ETERNITY CHANGES THE WAY WE ACT TODAY, AND THE WAY WE ACT TODAY CHANGES THE WAY WE SPEND ETERNITY.[4]

Somehow, I know that if I were in heaven I'd treat people differ-ently. There, I won't have to prove myself, explain myself, defend myself, keep myself safe, or even think of myself in the first place. Because I'll be in the presence of a knowing, loving, just, and beautiful

God. And the people I will interact with will be the best versions of themselves—loved and giving love like my eyes haven't seen. Seeing people in light of how we'll be for eternity makes me want to bring that same treatment and vision down here to earth. Eternity changes the way we act today, and the way we act today changes the way we spend eternity.[4]

Most times, the issues that come up in our relationships aren't eternal, Kingdom things. They will burn up when Christ returns. Album covers, clothing styles, five-minutes-late or five-minutes-early tendencies, denominations, colleges, and TP rolled under or over will all burn up. But love, joy, peace, patience, kindness, goodness, faithfulness, gentleness, and self-control—these things will not. They are the fruit of our eternal God. This doesn't mean those other things don't matter, it just means they are secondary pursuits. The Kingdom of God is our first. Ann Voskamp wrote, "Don't waste a minute on anything less than what lasts for all eternity."[5] As we plant seeds, let's do it with the great big love and vision of heaven.

I want to be clear: "What you sow is what you reap" is not saying the same thing as "Do it all right and God will make good things happen to you." As we talk about planting and harvesting, I'm not promising results. God is promising rewards according to the eternal economy of heaven. In that economy, what is least becomes greatest, what is unseen is applauded, success means losing our lives for His sake, and moving up means humbling ourselves. It is an economy where our surrendered sorrows become the wealth of heaven.

SEEDS OF SORROW AND DISAPPOINTMENT

You've probably seen girls who had relationships with their dads that you envied. Maybe you've had dreams your dad never noticed or encouraged. Or words of acceptance you longed for, but never heard from him. We all have dreams, ideals, and expectations, and we all face disappointment when those things don't happen. What are we supposed to do when we look around and see mighty oaks lining the lawn of the neighbor's home, and we look into our own hand to find only an acorn?

I can think of only one thing: plant it.

Every seed must die. If they don't, there will be no lasting, touchable, tastable fruit. To grow a harvest, there must be hundreds of tiny deaths underneath the tilled soil of the garden. The harvest comes only after the necessary process: tilling, planting, small deaths, microscopic growth, and then quiet waiting as plants grow in their own time.

You are free to feel those small deaths for what you didn't have. Grieve what you wish could be, but isn't. Be honest with the loss. The disappointments. The unfulfilled desires. Then place these losses, disappointments, and unfulfilled desires in the ground as an act of trust and surrender to your God. He cares about these dreams and ideas. But He knows the way His Kingdom works.

The way to life is always death. The way to grow up comes only after being put down. We probably won't heal if we don't grieve. We probably won't grow if we're not honest. We probably won't know the truth if we justify our dad's actions by comparing them to someone who has a more difficult situation. And we probably won't know the real God if we live in a fictional expectation.

Sometimes the most honorable action we can choose is letting things be just as they are for this moment. What if, today, you let your relationship with your dad be what it is—average or confusing or tragic? What if you didn't hope away your current reality or justify the ways that piercing thorns have choked this relationship? Jesus worked miracles when people came to Him as they were, in faith. Not when they had already figured it out, found medicine for their sickness, or shared their testimony of how their life turned out well. Jesus is the one who changes and writes stories, not us. Let the seed die, and see if your tear-watered earth will grow something new. Don't avoid what is hardest or least exciting, or you will have no garden at all.

Placing my dreams into the ground has taught me this Christ-centered, gospel way. Where the goal is relationship with the Father. Where the hope is the presence of God. Where the focus is on knowing Him. Facing our reality is not about giving up on our dreams and hopes. It's about the glory of our God instead of the story of our lives.

I like the way Lara Casey said it: "You have a unique assignment here on this earth, and your pain, grief, and challenges might be the very things that open your heart to be able to live out that assignment. A seed doesn't burst through the earth and decide to hop to another spot because it looks better, easier, or more comfortable in someone else's garden. It grows right in the dirt where it has been planted."[6]

In the Kingdom of God, nothing is wasted. Even our sorrows and disappointments can grow into an abundant harvest. In your planting, don't be surprised by the death of a seed. Don't walk away when you don't see results in your own heart or in your relationships. Stay, water, and watch for the growing God will do.

SEEDS OF ENCOURAGEMENT

I once heard our family friend Ken Yoder say, "Pick something about your dad that you like and tell him. I swoon when my daughters say something they like about me. When they do, I'm so touched I have to find a private corner to cry." Dads need our positive words too. They need to hear that they're fun to be around. They need some thanks and gratitude for the ways they provide and sacrifice for us more than we can even see.

"Out of the abundance of the heart the mouth speaks," says Matthew 12:34. Our words tell others what kind of roots are forming in our soil.

James 3 compares our words to a spring, an olive tree, and a fig tree. Verse 9 says with the same tongue we "bless our Lord and Father, and with it we curse people who are made in the likeness of God." If you're a fig tree, figs will grow on you. If you're a bitter spring, bitter water will come out of you. When we have the life of the Spirit as the ruler of our hearts, that whole, alive person will bring forth words of life. When our hearts are His, the way we communicate with our dads will change. Because what is inside us will come out.

In my relationships, I'm learning to give thanks for what is, instead of complaining about what isn't. Affirm, bless, encourage, and give thanks in the areas where your dad is doing things well. Recognize the places he has taught you something valuable about God and life. For instance, my dad isn't the best at initiating connection and conversation with me. He assumes that if I'm not asking to talk about something, everything is fine. Sometimes I've been hurt, feeling like I have to be the one to initiate connection between us.

I've had to learn to appreciate what my dad *does* do for connection. Even if my dad is a poor initiator, he is a great communicator when we do take time together. Instead of putting more pressure on him to initiate, it's important for me to thank him and speak well of the way I can have healthy, understanding conversations with him.

Maybe your dad is a workaholic. That isn't something to praise. But there's a good chance that, even in this weakness, he has taught you attributes of diligence and hard work. You don't have to mimic his obsession with work, but you can thank him and bless him for the positive life lessons he has taught in spite of his weakness.

Maybe your dad seems passive. This can make following his lead complicated. But there's a good chance he has also shown you gentleness and patience through his quiet personality. Bless these attributes instead of criticizing the ways you wish he would lead.

Many times, daughters feel like their dads judge them, don't understand them, or don't accept them for who they are. These are valid hurts. But to turn around and sow your own judgment, criticism, and rejection toward him will not yield the fruit of mercy, understanding, and acceptance in our lives. What we sow is what we will reap.

Speak words of life over your father's weaknesses and imbalances. Think about it: if your dad is critical and you criticize him for it, what are you? If your dad has a hard time leading out so you put expectations on him to be different, do you think that will encourage or discourage a desire to lead more? When we use our words for blessing instead of negativity about our dad's weaknesses, we are sowing encouragement instead of repaying them with the very attributes that bother us.

I'll be the first to admit, this concept comes hard for me. I tend to have high ideals and expectations in relationships, and I don't mind telling someone if they've failed to live up to them. God is causing a growth of gratitude in me for what I do have and what others do for me, slowly pruning out my ideals of how things could be better.

How would our relationships with our dads look if we loved them the way we want to be loved? If we gave mercy over judgment in the same way we want to receive mercy? What if we sowed into their garden what we want them to sow in ours?

SEEDS OF PRAYER

I have much to learn about prayer, especially intercession. Sometimes I find myself praying for people I love in an effort to control the outcome of their lives or character. This is praying with an agenda instead of praying from a relationship with Father God. When I pray, I am learning to ask Jesus what *He* is praying.

Jesus intercedes for us.[7] Remembering this melts me every time. Think of the involvement, intention, and care He has for each individual life. Prayer works when the things we speak are also the things He is speaking and saying over our lives and the lives of others. Prayer works when it aligns with His Word, His Spirit, and therefore His Will.

You can be a part of bringing Christ's Kingdom here on earth by agreeing with His heart and thoughts toward your dad and then speaking them into this world. I often fail to support my dad in prayer. I forget all he has on his plate and how the seeds of prayer can lift him to more grace as he fathers our family.

Oswald Chambers said this about prayer, "To say that 'prayer changes things' is not as close to the truth as saying, 'prayer changes me and then I change things.' God has established things so that prayer, on the basis of redemption, changes the way a person looks at things."[8] Prayer changes our perspective. Instead of noticing weaknesses, we begin to speak blessings in their place. If you notice your dad lacks patience, bless him with patience in your prayers. If you feel anger from your dad, speak love and gentleness over him in prayer.

More than anything, prayer is about being in the presence of God. In this next and final chapter, we will explore more ways to plant good seeds in the lives of our dads and see what happens in us and our relationships when we are saturated in the presence of God.

ACTING INTENTIONALLY

There have been times I intentionally prayed certain character traits over my dad. I remember once I prayed a simple prayer of blessing over a few specific attitudes. Days later, he ended up apologizing for the exact things I was praying over. I'm not sure why, but I was blown away when I actually saw this result.

If something is bothering you about your dad, try praying blessings over him. Make a list of the things you're praying for. Then just watch and see what God may want to do—in him or in you.

ASK YOURSELF

o   What are my sensitive spots? Where do I often react or shut down?

o   How have my dad's words affected me, positively or negatively?

o   Are there disappointments and sorrows in my relationship with my dad that I need to grieve over?

o   Are there words of thanks or affirmation I've failed to tell my dad?

THE BRAND OF LOVE
THAT JESUS OFFERS IS MORE ABOUT

presence

THAN UNDERTAKING A PROJECT.

BOB GOFF[1]

CHAPTER 9

home

HOW THE PRESENCE OF GOD CHANGES
THE ATMOSPHERE

I remember one Sunday when my pastor shared the story of a young businessman who stepped onto a public transportation bus for the first time in his life. Not many people used public transportation in the upscale part of town where the businessman worked, but today he decided he wanted to give it a try—do something different, shake up his routine. He handed the driver several dollars, then scanned the bus, finding only one man stationed on the back seat with his face hidden behind a newspaper.

The new passenger picked out his choice seat in the front row and mimicked the demeanor of the experienced passenger on the back seat, pulling out his paper and settling in for the ride. The bus made several stops in the nice part of the city, but soon it headed into an area that made the businessman lay down his paper and look out the window. Deteriorating brick buildings and unkempt homes contrasted with the new, well-kept buildings he'd seen only a few miles back.

But soon, more than his eyes were affected by this bus route. He placed his hand over his nose as the bus doors opened at yet another stop. The stench from the factories just outside the bus was suffocating.

Several factory workers boarding the bus looked at one another and smiled as they saw the grimacing face of the new passenger.

By now, the bus was more than half full with factory workers who reeked as much as their place of employment. One of the workers, who seemed to be in good spirits, chose the seat next to this new mystery passenger. The businessman attempted a polite nod through his tense face, and the factory employee returned the cold greeting with a tip of his hat and a smile too big for the circumstances. The factory worker must have noticed the businessman's obvious discomfort. "Not much longer yet, and we'll be in your part of town," he said.

The next stop held yet another batch of factory workers. The businessman tensed as the doors opened, preparing for the foul smell. But his brow furrowed when a surprisingly different aroma filled the bus. These workers were also dirty and unkempt, yet the bus instantly smelled of sweet perfume as they stepped on.

The factory worker couldn't help but laugh out loud at the perplexed expression on his fellow passenger's face. He offered an explanation to the businessman's unspoken question: "They work in the perfume factory."

The perfume-doused workers defused the grimace on the businessman's face, inviting him to take a deep breath and relax. What they were saturated in changed the fragrance of the atmosphere.

A bad smell can invade any space, making it uncomfortable and repulsive. There are actually quite a few things that can invade our senses and change an atmosphere: music that's too loud, an irritating noise, heat or cold that won't let us relax.

There are things in an atmosphere that invade not just our senses, but also our emotions. A cool remark can invade our security. The silent treatment from someone we love can invade our connection. Tense tones can invade peace in the room. A harsh glance can invade our sense of approval.

A good smell, on the other hand, creates an inviting atmosphere.

Our family gets welcomed into many people's homes as we travel, and there are few things more inviting than walking through someone's front door to the fragrance of a warm meal. My dad often breathes in deeply, then comments, "This smells like the place to be."

There are many things that invite our senses to feel alive and at rest: a bed covered in soft blankets after a long day of work, familiar food set on the family table, a slow walk through a quiet pine forest, or a rainy afternoon in a small cafe. They all seem to invite our senses home. Things in an atmosphere can also invite our emotions to higher and deeper expressions: a sonata can move us to tears, a wink across the room can make us blush, or a good joke can curl us into breathless laughter. A kind word can bring us alive, an understanding look can make us feel safe, and healthy conversation can give us connection.

Whatever atmosphere we're in, that place becomes marked by the things we experience there. The smells, sights, and emotions all create embedded memories, associations, and feelings that can't be easily undone. Some are good, and some are bad. The bad ones seem to invade our heart like a strong odor. When an atmosphere that should feel inviting and refreshing becomes an atmosphere that's stifling and unsettling, we feel especially violated by it. Like a gorgeous wedding venue downwind from a dairy farm, or a luxurious hotel room reeking with cigarette smoke. An atmosphere where we expect to experience good becomes a place we experience bad. This often happens in the place where we wish we would feel most safe, warm, and loved—our homes.

A SAFE HOME

"Each of us longs for a place to belong. A connection that gives roots to our wandering lives," says Sally Clarkson.[2] Everywhere I go, I find girls exploring this idea of belonging. I see their side glances at youth group hangouts. I hear their questions while piled up in my lamplit bedroom, wondering where they fit when they've moved a lot, or they don't have the same ideas as their friends, or they haven't always been able to trust people in their own homes. We all have a deep need for belonging. This need is amplified and more confusing when we haven't experienced the freedom, warmth, and safety of belonging in our own homes.

Home is meant to be the place where our best is called to life and where we are loved at our worst. It's supposed to be a safe place. Home is where we learn and grow and develop our talents, because it's the place we don't have to fear failure. It's the place where bad smells of underlying tension are dealt with instead of left to become normal. Where the mess of attitudes and mistakes are cleaned up in love instead of hidden in fear. It's the place for tears, laughter, and always knowing that no one will be left or rejected. Home smells like the place to be.

Because our dads are the heads of our homes, how we experienced them becomes tied to what we know about coming home. In a fallen world, these descriptions of home aren't everyone's reality. Many of us have been blessed with safe homes like this, and others have not always felt safe or loved in their homes. Either way, these descriptions help us understand what it means when we have been adopted into the household of God.

Our craving for belonging is actually a craving for where we were really meant to be. Don't be frustrated if this world leaves you longing for the place your DNA came from: heaven. We weren't meant to be here forever. Yet, even here, we are welcomed to enter the rest of God—a kind of home for our souls. It is an unseen home where we are freed to be ourselves in Him. Where we can learn, grow, try things, and fail without fear. Where there is a continual voice of love, tenderness, and joy in His presence.

When we know this kind of home in Christ, we will automatically begin to bring a different presence into the home we were chosen for on earth. Even if there are things about our home we can't change, people around us will smell what or who we've been around.

CHANGING YOUR ATMOSPHERE

One evening a few girlfriends and I were gathered together for a special summer dinner. My friend Abbie is the best at hosting parties, and she certainly didn't disappoint us that evening. She spread a table in her living room, clothed it with fresh summer decor, and whipped up the greatest array of beautiful food and drinks.

We talked casually, then deeply, then had random bouts of laughter. Floating from one subject to another, we eventually landed on the topic of our dads. Then someone threw out the idea that the way we treat our dads now could indicate how we will treat our husbands in the future.

The beautiful, recently engaged Kate flicked back her blonde bangs and said sarcastically, "But Dad just isn't as charming, hilarious, and adorable as Matt is. Surely, honoring my husband will be far easier than honoring my dad!"

We all laughed, relating more than we wanted to admit. Sometimes we have a castle-in-the-sky perspective about the wonderful women we will be in the future, but we don't think that woman will reach her full potential until charming, hilarious, adorable Matt comes along.

Or perhaps we think we will be better employees once we get a better boss, or a better Christian once we get a more Spirit-filled pastor. In reality, if we aren't living faithfully now—exactly where we're at with exactly what we have—by the time adorable Matt comes along, he may find a grumpy woman who doesn't attract him the way she hoped she would. Maybe once a new minister is ordained in the church, we will be the lay member he has a burden for because of the complacent Christian life we've been practicing. That new boss may be unimpressed with our bad work ethic produced by years of waiting for someone to notice our true potential.

If we can't be faithful now, who's to say we will be in that hypnotizing *someday?*

But I get it, the places that feel the most mundane—like home—can sometimes be the hardest to live out the beautiful gospel. Yet it is precisely who we are in these mundane places that determines who we will be on a larger platform.

When we encounter the gospel, we begin to live as though the things that are the least seen are the most important. How we relate to the untrophied, unnoticed, unrewarded parts of life defines who we are in the Kingdom of God. When everything inside us wants to focus on our image online, in church, in business, in school, or in youth group, the gospel reminds us to ask, "How do I treat the people in my home?"

I remember when one of my brothers started to change how he lived out the gospel at home. He's always been a nice brother, but sometimes I got the feeling that home wasn't his favorite place to be. But then I noticed a shift. I could tell he was experiencing new levels of growth and freedom in Christ. He was becoming more flexible with his opinions and more open with his schedule and plans. He was more pleasant, happy, and up for a good time. Everyone in the house began to feel more valued by him. We felt like he wanted to be with us. He would come home from work and ask my mom questions about her day and how she was doing. He was more grateful for various gestures done for him around the house. He honored others' thoughts more deeply.

Then an odd thing began to happen to me. I thought I was relating well with people at home, until he would get home. His presence and thoughtfulness made me see all the opportunities I had missed to love the people around me. I hadn't thought to ask them this question, or thank them for what they had done here or there. I had been driven in my schedule, while he was aware of the needs of those around him. I had missed opportunities to laugh or be silly or be grateful.

Sometimes we get so accustomed to feeling or smelling a certain way in a certain place that we miss ways the atmosphere could be different. All it takes is for someone else's positive, life-giving thoughts, presence, and gestures to show us how beautifully we could have been living in the same place.

This is what knowing Jesus can be like. When we receive His invitation to more—more joy, more life, more peace, more grace, more love, more holiness—our presence begins to invite others to more.

I believe women in particular carry the invitational nature of God. The ability to create an atmosphere where people experience the warmth, beauty, and wholeness of a moment in the presence of God. They create atmospheres in hearts and in physical places that invite and nurture.

Our presence as daughters in our father's house has the potential to invite or invade. I've invaded peace in our home through my rebellion. I've invaded rest in our home through pressured performance. I've invaded connection in our home through shutting down. And because my dad lives in my home with me, these things have invaded my relationship with him.

But we always have an opportunity to learn a new way in the nature of Christ. We can invite our dads into the presence of God. By the way we laugh. By the twinkle in our eye and the honor in our voice. By the way we dress around the house. In the music we turn on. In the plans we make for a good time. In the ways we are available to be helpful. All of this shows value to the people we don't normally try to impress.

> OUR PRESENCE AS DAUGHTERS IN OUR FATHER'S HOUSE HAS THE POTENTIAL TO INVITE OR INVADE.

If I always look grungy around the house, but put lots of effort into my clothes, hair, and makeup before I go to be with friends, does that show that I honor the people in my house? If I'm constantly making plans to do fun things with my friends, but I don't do anything intentional to build a deeper relationship with my dad, what does that say about my value for him?

Carrying the presence of God lifts the atmosphere of a home. And I'm learning we carry His presence best when we are freely, fully who He created us to be.

BEING YOURSELF IN YOUR HOME

I remember walking down our dead-end road on a beautiful spring day, my Bible open in my hand. I read aloud from Ephesians 5:1, "Be imitators of God, as beloved children." I wondered to myself, *What does it mean to imitate God?* Does that mean imitate the way my younger brother can imitate the voices, laughs, gaits, or facial expressions of anyone he meets? Or like an actor imitates the character he's playing—briefly becoming someone else? Is that the way we become like God?

No, it reads "imitators . . . as beloved children." Our imitation of Christ is not our ability to mimic Him in a way we can never sustainably copy. It's an imitation that comes from being around Him.

Children often act like their parents, even if they have completely different personalities and traits. They naturally relate, verbalize, and embody the expressions and gestures of their parents. Why? Because they've been around them since birth. They've looked into their parents' faces and watched their parents' responses and expressions. They didn't have to teach themselves to use their hands like their mom does or laugh like their dad. They were just with them.

When we are in the presence of God, we begin to become like Him. Ultimately, we lose sight of ourselves because we're watching Him. Then He turns around and talks to us about who we are and why He created us the way He did.

Our modern world manufactures, carbon copies, and machine makes, but our kind God does not. I don't want you to feel lumped into a particular type of acting, feeling, or thinking as a daughter. I want you to discover what it looks like to be *yourself* to your dad.

You are your father's daughter for a reason. You were individually chosen for the household you live in. He made you for your area, your family, and your dad, because He desires for you to uniquely express His character and worship Him in a way that literally no one else could.

If we try to influence, love, and affect our homes by being a certain type of forced "godly," instead of simply being who God made us to be, we may end up frustrated. I've had rocky days of trying to do just that.

A friend recently told me a story from when my little sister was in her Sunday school class years ago. The question was posed to the four-year-olds, "What is something hard in your life?" She must've been a deep teacher. I'm trying to imagine my hardships as a four-year-old.

I probably would have chosen a two-word answer: my younger brother's first and middle name. Turns out, my little sister used a sibling's name to answer the teacher too. It was mine. She said,

"Sometimes Deborah isn't nice to me."

The teacher was dumbfounded. At the time, she hardly knew me, and for some reason thought I was the epitome of virtue and patience (Lord knows I wanted to be). She joked that "mean" must simply have meant I forgot to kiss her goodnight sometimes or I didn't always smile when I spoke to her.

I rolled my eyes. If only that were the case.

I knew early on in my teen years that I wanted to actively invest in my home and the relationships in it. But I'd often get frustrated in the process. I was short-tempered, irritable, controlling, impatient, and overly sensitive in my home. There were times I felt overwhelmed by how bad I was at relating to the people closest to me. Even if my relationships were primarily healthy, I often found myself feeling trapped by my own bad attitudes.

It bothered me that I was inconsistent. My desire versus my reality was embarrassing. I wanted to be impactful. And I made an impact all right, but not in the way I'd planned. Looking back, I see a girl with good intentions going about it in all the wrong ways. I thought I could just learn better character, act nicer, and control my tense tones and quick reactions. C. S. Lewis said it well, "No man knows how bad he is until he has tried very hard to be good."[3]

Trying to improve our sin nature with better character will always be hard, impossible work. It's not until our sin nature dies and our souls are being led by the Spirit of God that things change. Then it is His nature that does the living and responding, and we begin to understand who we are in light of who He is.

Discovering who I am as an individual in my household has been an empowering tool to love the people within that household. When we're settled in who we are, we just become more fun. We laugh more, give more, and stress less. In fact, the best way to make life *not* about us is to become truly settled in who we are. Then we can celebrate others' strengths and gifts, and use our own even when they aren't perfect. We can even use our gifts when they're highly praised and still remain humble because they don't define us—God already has. Natural humility and worship come when we know who we are in Him. We don't have to deny our gifts, prove them, or downplay them. Because those things do not define who we are, they are just a part of how we uniquely express His workmanship in our lives.

We will affect the atmosphere in our home not because we do it all right or try to attain a certain kind of character. We will lift the atmosphere of our home by letting Christ be Himself through us, which, in ways I don't even understand, lets us be ourselves as He created us to be.

Your dad needs you to be you, whether he has told you or not. Recently, all the ladies in my pastor's family were away for the week on a girls' trip. I followed their adventures on Instagram and loved watching the grand time they were having together. At the end of the trip, the sweetest Facebook post popped up on my feed from their dad and husband. When they arrived home, he had roses waiting for them, each in a different, bright color. The Facebook caption read, "They bring so much color to our home."

Each of these girls is so different. One is pursuing missions overseas, one is engaged, two are moms, and another is working toward her bachelor's degree. Some are homebodies and objective thinkers, while others are spontaneous travelers and creative thinkers. Each brings a presence to their home like the others couldn't, and their dad knows that best.

We cannot follow someone else's model of how to be uniquely ourselves in our home. We will bring life to an atmosphere in our *own* skin. And in the same way, our dads were made to be our dads in their own skin.

ALLOWING OUR DADS TO BE THEMSELVES

We often create tension and confusion in our relationships when we require of others what God does not require of them. James 3:16 says, "For where envy and self-seeking exist, confusion and every evil thing are there" (NKJV). When we create expectations for our dads in order to serve our own self-seeking ideas, things get more complicated. Sometimes we look to stereotypes of what we think godly leaders should look like. We compare them to other models of manhood. When we measure their love by our own condition, we set them up for failure and miss the value of what God has given us in our personal dad.

Your dad doesn't need to have a bold, verbal personality to be a good leader. He doesn't have to have family devotions every night to be spiritual. He doesn't need to take you on dates to be thoughtful. He doesn't have to fit into your stereotypes in order to be heroic. We love it when our dads accept us the way we are, don't we? I think it's time we do the same to them.

It's valuable to know what makes your dad feel loved and respected. What is your dad's love language?[4] This may help you understand his efforts to love you, even when it feels like he's doing the opposite of what you want. Some dads may naturally speak your love language because theirs is the same. Others will, unknowingly, speak their own love language to you and misunderstand how you want to be loved. Let's give them grace here because we probably do the same to them more than we'd like to admit.

If you ever feel like it's difficult to give or receive love from your dad, it's helpful to remember that your dad is a man and you are not. It's also helpful to remember that your dad is a specific type of man with a signature personality and story. Learn about him. This helps you understand his way of thinking and how he relates to you. It also helps you understand why there may be some disconnections in your relationship. It can help you communicate your own needs, desires, and expectations instead of silently holding them in.

There are moments when your dad isn't doing anything wrong, he's simply doing something different from your expectations. Knowing this can keep you from treating him like he's a different species who hails from another planet. He is human, he is a man, and he is an individual created by God. It's helpful to remember this, treat him like this, and understand how his attributes can be a grace in your life, not a hindrance.

Learning about the unique ways you and your dad tick can be a rescue in your daily interactions. It also helps you know how to communicate expectations and desires. It may be helpful for you to have a conversation with your dad about what your own love language is and how he comes across to you because of the way you process or think. Then ask him how you can more accurately honor and enjoy him for who he is. Because you need your dad to be himself, whether you realize it or not.

SELF: SINFUL NATURE
OR REDEEMED IDENTITY

As we've been talking about being "ourselves," you may be wondering what in the world our "self" even is. There is a difference between who God created us to be and our sinful flesh. Being ourselves is not the same as letting our flesh rule our lives. Following our flesh makes for unhealthy, warped versions of what God intended us to be. Denying our flesh and following the Spirit of God frees us to be who God created us to be.

We often know who we want to be and how we want to act. We want to be fun, kind, humble, loving, enjoyable, and successful. We want to exemplify Christ's character. So then we feel a little set back when instead we're moody, impatient, unable to connect with others, or unable to consistently do what we want to do. Paul describes this battle in Romans 7:15, writing, "For I do not understand my own actions. For I do not do what I want, but I do the very thing I hate." We can all relate to this in some way, whether in our motivations, actions, thoughts, or attitudes.

Then Paul says, "So now it is no longer I who do it but sin that dwells within me. For I know that nothing good dwells in me, that is, in my flesh. For I have the desire to do what is right, but not the ability to carry it out" (verses 17–18).

Paul is acknowledging that the flesh is the sinful nature of Adam that he was born with. Our flesh has no long-term power to have Christlike character in our homes. This is why Jesus came to be the Second Adam.[5] He has come to replace this fleshly nature with His own nature, which frees Him to be Himself in us. When it comes to our flesh, we need to daily deny ourselves and follow Christ. The more dead our flesh is, the more alive He is in us. Then His nature in us sets us free to be who He created us to be.

This idea has transformed the way our family approaches personality differences and flaws. We have always been taught that our personality is never an excuse for sin or bad character. Yet in our home, it was obvious that we were all different. And it's sometimes hard to tell when different is wrong and when it's just . . . different.

My dad and I especially have had confusing pain surrounding our unique makeup. In my growing-up years, I began to believe that I was stupid, inconvenient, and high-maintenance compared to my dad's personality and traits. Our family's approach to character at that point tended to be focused on pointing out flaws in each other.

But before I even became a teenager this began to shift. When my dad noticed flaws in our character, he began to focus more on calling out who we were created to be in Christ than on highlighting how we were failing to live up to it. Our family is still in the process of learning how to honor the differences in our home instead of being bothered by them. We are learning to be intentionally verbal when we see good traits in each other, calling out who that person was created to be.

My dad and I went through some tough seasons as we grappled with the labels we had placed on each other due to our individual personalities and tendencies. I often made him the bad guy with his too many cautions, red flags, and logic overloads. These labels created some hard barriers to our connection. And the labels he placed on me caused some major pain.

Here's the thing: both of us saw necessary ways the other needed to grow. Both of us saw bad character and attitudes in each other. There's nothing wrong with that. But when we approach bad character with more bad character, we will hurt the other person. When we address a lack of Christlikeness with an equal lack of Christlikeness, we are simply in a battle of two sin natures. But when we address the issues we see in others by calling out who we know Christ made them to be, even if it includes some hard words, then life will come instead of pain and truth will come instead of more lies.

My dad and I are learning not to place labels on each other that aren't true about our identity in Christ. Whenever we use the words "you are . . ." we try not to follow them up with a statement that contradicts who they are in Christ. Making statements like *you are insensitive, you are too emotional, you are stubborn, or you are always overreacting* declares that there is something wrong with the person, instead of addressing that something is wrong with their attitude or actions.

Instead, we try to ask questions to understand why the other may be reacting. We are learning to address the attitude or action without stating that these attitudes and actions define who the person is. It's okay to say things like: *This is how you came across to me* or *I feel dishonored when you act this way.* It's okay to confront unhealthy attitudes or address spaces where you see room for growth.

When we address issues that result from our sinful nature, we have to remember how Father God looks at us. When He sees us, He smiles on the born-again nature of His perfect Son in us. Yet He graciously convicts us when we aren't walking in alignment with His nature.

With my dad, I am still learning what it looks like to smile on who he is in Christ. It's so easy for me to forget the value of the people around me. Today, let's remember our dads were created in the image of God to express Him uniquely. We are free to have honest conversations about differences and wrongs, but let's not dishonor the life of Christ inside them or devalue the image they were created in. Let the scale of affirming to corrective words be heavy on the affirmation. This frees them and us to be ourselves, instead of fearfully wondering if our signature selves will be unaccepted or put in a box.

Sometimes home becomes the place where being "ourselves" is unsafe, targeted, and stereotyped. But if we allow God to define us and begin to let Him define our views on the people in our home, we may help change the culture of how to handle the clear flaws that come through our sin nature.

You may wonder, *How do we let God define us individually? How do I know how He feels about me?* Even if we know we're His girls, sometimes we wonder how He feels about our personality, our gifts (or lack thereof), and the nuances of our habits and ways. Even people's nice words to us don't compare to hearing the Spirit of God talk to us about who we are. That is my simple recommendation and my continual process. Looking at Him. Letting His Word define me. Listening for His voice.

I like the way Jackie Hill Perry said, "We don't find out about ourselves by looking at ourselves; Eve didn't take the fruit because she had low self-esteem, but because she didn't believe who God was." Jackie followed up with this powerful statement: "Do you believe who God says He is? And if so, believe Him when He says who you are."[6] Our first misconceptions about ourselves often come from our misconceptions about our Father God. Who He is makes us who we are.

Home is meant to be a place where people are constantly called to life. Where honest correction and counsel are done in love. Where differences are celebrated. Where people are free to be themselves and honored for the unique way they bring the presence of God into the home. This kind of home is a picture of what it's like to be a part of the household of God.

Does the way you relate in your home make it obvious that you have been in the presence of God? That you dwell with God? We will live like Him because we dwell with Him, not just because we know all the right things to do. And when we begin to dwell as loved daughters in His house, our presence

> OUR FIRST MISCONCEPTIONS ABOUT OURSELVES OFTEN COME FROM OUR MISCONCEPTIONS ABOUT OUR FATHER GOD.

becomes an invitation to others to enter into the activity, joy, peace, and life that we can all experience within His household.

I don't know what it is for you. Maybe it's honesty, or using more encouraging words, or giving thoughtful gifts, or going out of your way to serve. It could be writing a note or making a phone call. But in some new way, try coming home with perfume on. Even if it's awkward. Even if it's odd because it's never been done. It may just be that what you're saturated in will affect the culture in your home and the next generations.

ACTING INTENTIONALLY

When I asked my dad if there was something I could do that would mean a lot to him, he said, "This isn't anything you do for me. But I'm most blessed when I just see you light, carefree, and laughing." How simple. We often bless others most when we are freely who God made us to be.

So be silly, lighthearted, and weird. Don't take yourself too seriously. Wear something nice around the house or light a candle for no special reason. Make your dad's favorite food. If you still live in your family home, remember you have a limited amount of days there. Live them intentionally. Fully, freely enjoy every day that God gives you with your dad.

The way we bring the presence of God into our homes may just be a picture of how God wants to use His daughters to impact the world.

ASK YOURSELF

- Am I trying to build my own character and identity on my flesh, or am I letting Christ live His nature through me?

- What can I intentionally do to create fun in my home?

- Am I allowing my dad to be himself?

- How could I use my God-given personality to affect the atmosphere of my home?

- Are there labels I have put on my dad that I need to tear off? Are there labels my dad has put on me that I need to tear off?

- What am I doing to intentionally spend time in the presence of God and saturate myself in His Word?

acknowledgments

This project has been a place of deep growth for me. There are few things I've done that have felt as risky, stretching, or unknown as writing a book. If it wasn't for the people around me, there would've been about 572 times I would've quit, published with a ghost name, or fled the country. Simply put, they wouldn't let me.

Without these people, I don't know if I would have believed God has something to say through me, nor would I have had the endurance and capability to finish what I started. With them, I have grown and known love and support of the extraordinary kind. I want to take a moment to thank them.

To Janessa, editor and developmental extraordinaire . . . thank you for every 2 a.m. night you pulled to reach deadlines, every long day in cafes hashing out ideas, every Vox and phone call, every word you edited, every time you listened to me rant or process when we should have been working, and every calm word you spoke into me as I navigated writing a book for the first time. Your presence in my process has felt like a divine gift from the hand of God.

To Emily Smucker . . . thanks for hopping into this project for objective feedback and line editing. You were just what we needed.

To the Gospel Express Executive Board and co-directors . . . thank you for your support, counsel, and wisdom. If every person had men of honor who believed in them, equipped them, and walked with them like you all have with me, this world would be a different place.

Thank you to my family for being a constant voice of life in this process. Most everything talked about in this book has come from the gift of having relationships with you all. I cannot find enough words of gratitude for how each of you have impacted my life and shown me Christ.

Thanking Jesus can feel trite, because of course He's the only reason for all of this! But when considering who I would thank and why I would thank them, it was the thought of what I would say to Him that, yet again, had me in tears of worship and thanks.

Jesus . . . thank You for being so near and warm. Thank You for loving me in a way that freed me to try something hard and maybe be totally wrong or ill-equipped, yet still be promised that You were with me. You have been bigger and able when I have not been. Thank You for grace. Thank You for how Your Word reveals Your character and ways. You have used this process to show me Yourself in a way I never knew You, and I am so grateful. Thank You for the Cross that made me a daughter of God. I hope I never get over that.

CHAPTER NOTES

CHAMPION:
a note to the daughters who have been misused, abused, or manipulated

1. Moore, Beth. *Audacious*. Nashville, TN: B&H Publishing Group, 2015.
2. This references the story of the Fall of Man, found in Genesis 3.
3. This references Jesus in the Garden of Gethsemane, as found in Matthew 26:36–46, Luke 22:39–46, and Mark 14:32–42. His subsequent death is found in the chapters following.
4. This scene is from the film *Anne of Green Gables*. Sullivan Entertainment, 1985.

CHAPTER 1
Father: a God who named Himself that

1. Chan, Francis. *Crazy Love: Overwhelmed by a Relentless God*. Colorado Springs: David C Cook, 2013.
2. Tozer, A. W. *The Knowledge of the Holy: The Attributes of God*. New York: HarperOne, 1978.
3. Kassain, Mary A. "Father of the Fatherless." *Journal for Biblical Manhood and Womanhood*, 2000. https://www.galaxie.com/article/jbmw04-4-05.

4. Chan, Francis, and Lisa Chan. *You and Me Forever: Marriage in Light of Eternity*. San Francisco: Claire Love Publishing, 2014.

5. From 2 Corinthians 1:3–5, "Blessed be the God and Father of our Lord Jesus Christ, the Father of mercies and God of all comfort, who comforts us in all our affliction, so that we may be able to comfort those who are in any affliction, with the comfort with which we ourselves are comforted by God. For as we share abundantly in Christ's sufferings, so through Christ we share abundantly in comfort too."

6. Keller, Timothy. *The Prodigal God: Recovering the Heart of the Christian Faith*. New York: Penguin, 2016.

7. Ibid.

CHAPTER 2
Communication: learning to connect with our dads

1. The idea behind this quote is original with Amos Raber: "Don't criticize your dad, be thankful for the things he did right, stand on his shoulders and build up from there."

2. Coblentz says this concept is taken from John 13:35: "By this all people will know that you are my disciples, if you have love for one another."

3. Farrance, Kirsteen. "Myths and Facts: Relays." *Athletics Victoria*, February 2, 2015. http://athsvic.org.au/2015/officials/myths-and-facts-relays-by-kirsteen-farrance/.

CHAPTER 3
Goodness: how delight and discipline affect our souls

1. Tozer, A. W. *Renewed Day by Day: A Daily Devotional*. Camp Hill: Christian Publications, 1991.

2. Chambers, Oswald. *My Utmost for His Highest*. Grand Rapids: Discovery House, 2017.

3. From 1 Corinthians 6:19–20, "Or do you not know that your body is a temple of the Holy Spirit within you, whom you have from God? You are not your own, for you were bought with a price. So glorify God in your body."

4. Leaf, Caroline. "Episode #52, What is the Mind/Brain Connection?" *Cleaning up the Mental Mess with Dr. Caroline Leaf.* Podcast audio, October 28, 2018. http://podcast.drleaf.com/e/ episode-52-what-is-the-mind-brain-connection/.

5. Rainey, Dennis. "Life Skills for the Art of Parenting: Giving Your Child a Biblical Identity (Sexual and Spiritual) and Releasing Your Child for His Mission." Session at Equipping Families to Stand Conference, Creation Museum, Petersburg, KY, July, 2018.

6. From Psalm 105:4, "Seek the LORD and His strength; Seek His face evermore!" (NKJV).

CHAPTER 4

Processing: understanding our childhood beliefs and present reactions

1. Concepts from this chapter taken from Ed Smith and Transformation Prayer Ministry. https://www.transformationprayer.org/.

2. From Romans 8:38–39, "For I am sure that neither death nor life, nor angels nor rulers, nor things present nor things to come, nor powers, nor height nor depth, nor anything else in all creation, will be able to separate us from the love of God in Christ Jesus our Lord."

3. These concepts can be found in 1 John 4:7-8, "For love is from God, and whoever loves has been born of God and knows God. Anyone who does not love does not know God, because God is love," and verse 18, "There is no fear in love, but perfect love casts out fear. For fear has to do with punishment, and whoever fears has not been perfected in love."

4. Wakefield, Norm. Spirit of Elijah Ministries. http://www.spiritofelijah.com/.

5. The Bible Hub website states, "The root of 4102/*pistis* ("faith") is 3982/*peithô* ("to persuade, be persuaded"), which supplies the core-meaning of faith ("divine persuasion")." *HELPS Word-studies*. https://biblehub.com/greek/4102.htm.

6. From 1 Kings 19:12, "And after the earthquake a fire; but the LORD was not in the fire: and after the fire a still small voice" (KJV).

7. From Zephaniah 3:17, "The LORD your God in your midst, The Mighty One, will save; He will rejoice over you with gladness, He will quiet you with His love, He will rejoice over you with singing" (NKJV).

CHAPTER 5

Submission: the brave heart of a daughter

1. Voskamp, Ann. *The Broken Way: A Daring Path into the Abundant Life*. Grand Rapids: Zondervan, 2016.

2. The story of Esther referenced throughout this chapter is found in the book of Esther in the Bible. The quotations on this page are taken from Esther 1:17, 19–20.

3. Ludy, Eric. "Reminders from Joshua Harris" series. *Daily Thunder*. Podcast audio, August 11–16, 2019. https://ericludy.com/eric-ludys-podcast-series-on-joshua-harris/.

4. Some verses showcasing God's heart for orphans: Psalms 10:14; 68:5; Deuteronomy 10:18; James 1:27.

5. From Ephesians 1:5, "He predestined us for adoption to himself as sons through Jesus Christ, according to the purpose of his will."

6. From Esther 4:16, "Then I will go to the king, though it is against the law, and if I perish, I perish."

7. From Ephesians 5:22, "Wives, submit to your own husbands, as to the Lord;" Ephesians 6:1, "Children, obey your parents in the Lord, for this is right;" and Ephesians 6:7, "Rendering service with a good will as to the Lord and not to man."

CHAPTER 6

Honor: how attitude affects our dreams

1. Elliot, James, and Elisabeth Elliot. *The Journals of Jim Elliot*. London: Pickering and Inglis, 1979.

2. Evans, Richard L. *Richard Evans Quote Book*. Salt Lake City: Publishers Press, 1976.

3. The story of twelve-year-old Jesus in the temple can be found in Luke 2:41–52.

4. This concept can be found in Matthew 18:2–3, "And calling to him a child, he put him in the midst of them and said, 'Truly, I say to you, unless you turn and become like children, you will never enter the kingdom of heaven.'"

5. This concept can be found in Hebrews 6:1–3, "Therefore let us leave the elementary doctrine of Christ and go on to maturity. . ."

6. Perry, Jackie Hill. "The Truth About Ourselves." From *Revive Our Hearts*, 2018. https://www.reviveourhearts.com/events/true-woman-18/message-3-truth-about-ourselves/.

7. The story of Joseph can be found in Genesis 37–50.

CHAPTER 7

Hero: honoring our dads even when we disagree with them

1. The concept of love languages is from: Chapman, Gary D. *The Five Love Languages: The Secret to Love That Lasts*. Chicago: Northfield, 2010.

CHAPTER 8

Growth: moving past avoiding bad into planting good

1. Casey, Lara. *Cultivate: A Grace-Filled Guide to Growing an Intentional Life*. Nashville: Thomas Nelson, 2017.

2. Melchizedek's priesthood is described in the following Scriptures: Genesis 14:18–20; Psalms 110:4; Hebrews 5:6, 10; Hebrews 6:20; Hebrews 7:1–17.

3. Prayer generally attributed to Jonathan Edwards.

4. Concept taken from John Bevere's sermon "Driven by Eternity." Faith Family Church, October 19, 2016. https://www.youtube.com/watch?v=S9X62XcSEN8.
5. Voskamp, Ann. *The Broken Way*, 2016.
6. Casey, Lara. *Cultivate*, 2017.
7. From Romans 8:34, "Who is to condemn? Christ Jesus is the one who died—more than that, who was raised—who is at the right hand of God, who indeed is interceding for us."
8. Chambers, Oswald. *My Utmost for His Highest*, 2017.

CHAPTER 9
Home: how the presence of God changes the atmosphere

1. Goff, Bob. *Love Does: Discover a Secretly Incredible Life in an Ordinary World.* Nashville: Thomas Nelson, 2014.
2. Clarkson, Sally. *The Lifegiving Home: Creating a Place of Belonging and Becoming.* Carol Stream: Tyndale Momentum, 2016.
3. Lewis, C. S. *Mere Christianity.* New York: Simon and Schuster, 1996.
4. Chapman, Gary. *The Five Love Languages,* 2010.
5. This concept is from 1 Corinthians 15:45, "Thus it is written, 'The first man Adam became a living being'; the last Adam became a life-giving spirit."
6. Perry, Jackie Hill. "The Truth About Ourselves." *Revive Our Hearts,* 2018.

GOSPEL EXPRESS MINISTRIES

At the heart of Gospel Express Ministries lie the themes of Compassion, Evangelism, and Discipleship. Compassion ministry includes the call of Christ in Matthew 25 "unto the least of these" who have physical needs. Family teams, music, and preaching serve as a priority in presenting the gospel message of hope. The United States and Canada, along with the country of Uganda, Africa, serve as our primary geographical focus. In addition, we periodically minister in the countries of Ghana, Nigeria, Kenya, Mexico, Belize, and India.

Gospel Express was founded in 1984 and is a non-profit 501-c3 faith based ministry and is funded by donations from generous individuals, businesses, and churches.

"Go therefore and make disciples of all the nations."
Matthew 28:19a

Fulfilling the Great Commission Through:

- Prison Services and Crusades
- Church Ministry/Revival Meetings
- Community Tent Crusades
- International Ministry
- Discipleship Seminars
- Bible Study Correspondence Courses
- Bibles and Discipleship Materials
- Singspirations
- Resources – CDs, DVDs, Books

To order resources or contact Gospel Express:
Phone – 828-859-7003
Email – mail@gospelexpress.com
Website – www.gospelexpress.com

about the author

Deborah Miller is 25 years old and lives with her parents and four siblings in the foothills of the North Carolina Blue Ridge Mountains. There she enjoys her sweet community and practices photography and event decor as side hustles. Hosting Bible studies and girls groups is her favorite part of every week she spends at home. For six months of the year, she travels with her family and Gospel Express Ministries, playing harp, singing, speaking, and sharing the 40 foot bus that takes them to prisons, churches, and communities across America. This family-style ministry allows them to meet new people, share on family life and discipleship, and evangelize in unique settings varying from prison cells to open air meetings in the red dirt of Africa. Deborah especially loves the women's events and international travels she gets to be involved in.

This book is a first-time project for Deborah, flowing out of a desire to be faithful with the opportunities that come from meeting people, hearing their stories, and learning to understand her own.

SAY HELLO!

CONTACT DEBORAH
deborah@gospelexpress.com

SEND A NOTE
Gospel Express
PO Box 217 • Lynn, NC 28750

CONTINUE THE CONVERSATION
GirltoGirlconversation

FOLLOW THE MILLER
FAMILY'S ADVENTURES
miller.family7